Restore Our Democracy

The Case for Equality and Justice

WERNER NEFF

Impressum

ISBN-13 for the printed book: **978-1-64999-089-1**

ISBN-10 for the printed book: **1649990891**

Kindle e-book ISBN: **978-1-64999-090-7**

Table of Contents

"In a tyranny, what you have to cultivate in the people is the capacity to fear. In a monarch, you have to cultivate a taste and capacity for honor. But in a republic, what has to be cultivated more than anything else is virtue, public virtue."

Charles-Louis de Secondat,
Baron de la Brède et de <u>Montesquieu</u>,
The Spirit of the Laws, 1748

Prologue

The United States, Motherland of Democracy

The United States of America is the motherland of modern democracy. Through the secession from the British Crown in 1776 and the establishment of a separate state, democratic principles were implemented in the structure of the United States government.

Subsequently, the Declaration of Independence and the American Constitution provided the model for the worldwide social upheavals of the 19th and 20th centuries. The Founding Fathers had analyzed the principles of the Athenian and Roman worlds, and integrated those with the milestones of governance from the Old World—such as the Magna Carta Libertate of 1215 and the Bill of Rights of 1689 in England, the ideas of John Locke, and Montesquieu's principle of separation of powers. Those philosophies were the foundation of the new nation. The main concern of the founders was to avoid tyranny.

The Constitution is still relevant and highly respected today. What is missing is the politicians' commitment to follow the country's basic ideals, which is to represent all Americans, rich and poor, white and colored, and healthy and sick. The country's leadership is allowing itself to be derailed and distracted from the essential business by needless quarreling at the highest levels of government. The vast differences between the ruling parties and their commitment creates desperation and resignation amongst the people and it leaves them helpless. We are left with this: the wealthy and the big corporations are ruling this country.

The primary reason we elect political officials is to manage the country and serve its citizens. The welfare of citizens and their protection is the responsibility of a democratic government. In other words, the legislators are responsible for orchestrating economic and political development that will secure safety and wellbeing, and a basic lifestyle for all American citizens, including the needy.

The world is divided into geographical and political areas. One of them is the Western World, which consists of the United States, Canada, a big part of Europe, Australia, and New Zealand. The leader of this conglomerate has been the United States of America ever since the end of WWII. The rebuilding of Europe, the profound changes in lifestyle, the invention and manufacturing of new products and services resulted in the Pax Americana, which is the most successful period in history, the post-war boom.

The United States, the biggest partner in the Western World, leading with a strong economy, has been losing authority during the past thirty years. I believe that the two party-quarreling, the tremendous efforts spent on self-promotion for the elections, and endless blaming and shaming of leaders weakens the country and takes away power and credibility. Because we are so focused on national politics and partisan winning, we cannot see the huge impact this weakness has on world politics. We have lost recognition and trust as a world leader.

What Inspired me to Write this Book?

What was the motivation to research the current state of the Nation and our democracy?

In 1848, the Swiss people copied its republican government structure with democratic rules from the United States of America. The two-chamber legislature is serving the well-being as well as the views of pluralistic and liberal societies with federalist, republican democracies. Strong economic relations and a reciprocal understanding of values and structure lead to the title of Sister Republics. The last time this was mentioned was in 2006.

During my studies in political science and economics, I recognized my deep love and commitment for democracy. The political and economic issues this country is facing motived me to use my background and experience to do research on the American democracy and its current situation. A Swiss citizen, I have been living in the U.S. for a decade now, and I have come to love the American people and this beautiful country. I am a resident with heart and soul, and I am deeply invested in the wellbeing of this country and its people to whom this book is meant as a contribution and inspiration. It is my fondest wish that the history and the democratic principles as well as my conclusive call for action will help strengthen our democracy.

Part 1: Concepts—Freedom, Republic, Democracy

Freedom First

Freedom is the driving force in American thinking and acting. It began with a desire to have a say in determining taxes, demands that were consistently rejected by the King in London.[1] The King refused to agree to the laws put forth by the colonies, making his consent to such laws conditional on the waiver of parliamentary rights by the colonists. Indirectly, the King hindered the work of the colonial parliaments, and often dissolved them to make his point. In turn, this was hindering the administration of justice and made it difficult for other colonials to immigrate.

Ultimately, there was only one way to freedom: separation from the British crown and the founding of the United States of America, based on the colonist's understanding of freedom. The resulting establishment of the new country using the principles of republican and democratic rules was a milestone in human history.

The Greek philosopher, Aristotle, called freedom the most important quality of democracy and named three conditions that must be present for freedom: autonomy, *i.e.,* self-legislation; originality, *i.e.,* legislators must originate from the country in

1 The details in this part are based on Daniel N. Robinson, *American Ideals: Founding a "Republic of Virtue"*, The Great Courses, Chantilly, VA, 2004

question; self-sufficiency, *i.e.,* that legislators should come from within the country. He added that freedom must not create new foreign dependencies.

The American history proves: Living in freedom leads to the development of creative ideas and opportunities. Freedom to invent and create must be open to everyone. This new idea, this new way of thinking gives rise to an abundance of lifestyles and economic development. Everyone is invited to make use of this freedom and to create and shape their lives as they desire.

Monarchy vs. Republic

Monarchy is the world of a kingdom. The King or Queen—the monarch—ruled in the Middle Ages his or her country and its people as he wished and at her discretion. That their orders were followed across a country was only possible with the help of a structure of subordination of nobles through a system called vassalage. A fief was the central element of feudalism.

The highest level in the hierarchy, the monarch, ruled over the entire kingdom, commanded the military, ruled the administration, and had the right to collect taxes and specific economic privileges. The first level of nobles received delegated rights and privileges, with obligations such as serving in the military, providing solders, or serving in the government. The first level of nobility delegated parts of these prerogatives to the second level of nobility. The subordination went on to the next level of the hierarchy and so forth. This was a sophisticated system of delegation of power and subordination well-known in medieval Europe.

The monarchy was the living expression of a class-based hierarchy, the aristocratic world. How one's life unfolded was predetermined by an individual's belonging to one of three classes: the priesthood/clergy, the nobility, and then all others: the people. On the basis of a person's birth, they were assigned a place in society. Even a clever mind would struggle to change his social position.

The opposite of the monarchy is the **Republic**. In it, offices are given to people whose exercise of power is limited in time, and whose exercise of that power is determined according to laws that are derived from the will of the people.

In place of the three-tier state, as it existed in pre-revolutionary France, with the absolute dominance of the aristocracy came the new rule by the vast majority of the people, commonly referred to as "popular rule", and a life based on democratic principles. Privileges on account of birth (aristocracy) and the representation of God (clergy) no longer possessed meaning.

What is Democracy?

Democracy is a structure of government, a political order or political system, in which power and government come from the people. This can be done directly, through a gathering of voters, or through a selection of representatives who make decisions on behalf of the people. The legitimacy to govern comes from the people and not from God or an ideal being, as we know from history.

The word "democracy" comes from ancient Greek, with "demos" referring to the people of the state and "kratos" meaning "violence" or "power". Cleisthenes, a Greek legal scholar and politician, is seen as the father of Athenian democracy. Athens and Sparta were the two leading city-states in ancient Greece and dominated the politics of the region in the 5th century B.C. In 510, Sparta helped the Athenians overthrow the unpopular tyrant, Hippias, and wanted to appoint a regent endorsed by Sparta in his place. Cleisthenes resisted this and turned toward the ideas of popular rule.

Thus, in 508 B.C., for the first time in human history, not a King or tyrant was installed, but a democratic structure of government was created. It did not meet today's expectations of democracy, as the right to vote was limited, and only men older than 30 were eligible to be elected as civil servants. Nevertheless, it was a start.

Forms of Democracy

In a democracy, people elect the legal representatives of government—and they have the legitimacy to vote them out. Furthermore, it is the people themselves who pass the laws directly or through their elected representatives.

Thus, democratic participation can be exercised directly or indirectly: the people can elect a parliament, which then passes the laws—this is known as "representative democracy". Alternatively, the people can directly elect the government (*e.g.*, by electing the President) and/or decide on laws through referenda—this is "direct democracy".

Free and fair elections of representatives are an essential criterion for every democracy. In most countries, including in the United States at the Federal level, the electorate has the right to vote into office or reject the elected representative. That is the only way to express, legally, approval or rejection of a political view. Indirect forms of disagreement like signed petitions, street demonstrations, or court litigations may influence the legislator.

Direct democracy—which only exists today at the national level in Switzerland, and, to a lesser extent in Australia, and in some states in the U.S.—is largely exercised through ballot boxes. In this country some townships and counties use town hall meetings to make municipal decisions. The founding fathers were concerned that forms of direct democracy could lead to a "tyranny of the majority", which is why this form of democratic participation is not used at the Federal level.

There are also many mixed forms of direct and indirect democracy. For example, a plebiscite will be held in France on a particular question, usually on a matter put forward by the President. In practice, however, these plebiscites are rare.

"In Switzerland, without the need to register, every citizen receives ballot papers at home and an information brochure for each vote (and can send it back by mail). Switzerland has a direct democracy system and votes (and elections) are organized about four times a year. (For example) Berne's citizens, in November 2008 (voted to elect or approve) about 5 national, 2 cantonal, 4 municipal referenda, and 2 (other) elections (government and parliament of the City of Berne) all at the same time."[2]

2 The voice of an anonymous resident of Berne, Switzerland. Please note that every inhabitant must register in the community when moving there. Rights and duties are derived from this registration, such as attending public school for children, tax liability, and for Swiss citizen: military or civilian service and election and voting rights.

While republic and monarchy are opposites, both forms of government can exist with or without democracy. While there is a royal family in a constitutional monarchy, the King or Queen has no or only limited power; he or she has—primarily or exclusively—representative functions, while government affairs are carried out by an elected parliament and an elected leader of the parliament. European examples include the royal families of Great Britain, the Scandinavian countries, Belgium, The Netherlands, and Spain.

Conversely, a republic can also be completely undemocratic, if it does not have the corresponding democratic institutions, or if it perverts them, as was and is the case in Communist party dictatorships. Leaders of such republics call themselves people's democracies, yet, in fact, there is no sign of real democracy in those cases.

Democracy as *Structure* and *Substance*

As a concept, democracy can be subdivided into *structure* and *substance*. The functioning of democracy is regulated by its laws, and it guarantees a free press, free discussion, the liberty to found and/or join an association, as well as the separation of power (legislation – administration – judiciary) and more.

Laws, in this sense, are formal requirements to allow elections to be held correctly: the determination of the constituencies, locations of the polling stations, opening times, the correct counting of votes, and correct forwarding and reporting of the results. The *structure* of a democracy is governed by the written rules and guarantees of personal freedoms, as well as the separation of powers within the government.

The "*structure*" stands for the formal, procedural half of democracy. Correct ballot procedures, correct counting of votes, correct identification of the constituents, the organization of the voting process—these conditions must be fulfilled to achieve a democratically elected Congress, *i.e.*, a democratic process.

Democracy is not only the organizing part of political life for the election. Democracy is as well an idea, an ideology, a concept, and values. This is the content, the *substance* of democracy. It consists of judgment, the theory, the spiritual values, the rules used in everyday life. These notions are in your heart and your brain.

True supporters of democracy must be very tolerant, and this includes accepting opposing viewpoints as an enriching experience and a challenge. The diversity of ideas among citizens must be used to find solutions that benefit the entire country and all its residents. Shifting from conservative to progressive thinking and back is not a failure—rather, it is an expression of democracy, which is always a balancing act between different opinions and values.

Misconception of Democracy

In my opinion, in the minds of most U.S. citizens, democracy is limited today to the structural process of elections, and the activities of majority-building for the passage of legislation. This, in and of itself, is a severe underestimation of the truth. The full functioning of democracy is in the interaction of *structure* and *substance*.

For example, many party members only see the right to vote as a good thing if it fits their own party's outcome. The same right is not recognized for the opposed party. In an open statement, a party member even admitted that it was all about "voter suppression", a suppression of the voters' will.[3] This in effect means that the election process has degenerated into a sheer demonstration of power.

Today it is evident that the formal requirements of democracy have turned into a problem for the *structure* of democracy. The rules for the organization of elections reveal many conflicts of interests. That is, many such rules support two contradictory values: democracy, which unequivocally supports the idea of "one person, one vote," and its opposite, the restriction of voting rights. All too often today, party preferences now play a greater role in electoral preparations than respect for democratic principles.

Perhaps it is simply too tempting to exploit others for your own advantage. Or, perhaps, if conflicts of interest are not recognized at the political level, this must be due to a lack of understanding of the idea of democracy—which is, again, comprised of both, *structure* and *substance*. When party politicians bask in the results of their electoral victories ("We have the agenda", stating that this party likes to govern alone), or when voting restrictions are sought to the detriment of the other party (voting only with a mandatory photo ID is "going to kick Democrats in the butt")[4], Americans show a lopsided understanding of democracy focused on structure. Something is missing. That something is *substance,* the concept for democratic values.

Here is an example of structure and substance of democracy: a state wants to introduce a mandatory requirement to vote only

---

3 Jason Sattler, "6 Other Times Republicans Admitted Voting Restrictions Are Just About Disenfranchising Democrats", *The National Memo,* October 25, 2013.

4 *Ibid.*

with a document equipped with photo ID. This is a formality, a part of structure. The state government has to realize this demand of the state legislator. Democratic substance means the state government has the intention and is following a certain procedure to grant a photo ID to all citizens of the state with easy access to authorized offices, in close proximity to all populated areas, and generous opening hours. By contrast, it is undemocratic (what happened in Alabama 2015), when the state legislator decided to invent a mandatory photo-ID as a voting card and closed the number of driving license offices at the same time (see p. 118). This is a crime against democracy and should be punished. The reason is a complete lack of democratic substance.

Principles of Democracy

A Democracy is a community that finds a common basis through dialog, to manage everyday life in harmony and to tackle problems collectively. The coexistence and juxtaposition of different opinions, and the formulation of common goals, represent the core challenges of democracy as a form of government. Solutions are often a compromise—a third solution between the extremes. Majority and minority must come together in the spectrum of opinions. The existence of different opinions and values is not the problem, but the norm. Observing these rules is considered democratic. It is a democratic principle to strike a balance between the different population groups.

Democracy is generosity, a life full of compromises, a state of constant readjustment, a life in balance. However, this is only possible if one does not regard the political opponent as an enemy; they must be a partner whose ideas have to be brought in so that a consensus can be reached. The perfect democracy is a constant effort to bring different values together.

This picture of democracy is an ideal; it shows that there are established forms of political governance. The United States has been demonstrating the benefits of this system for over 200 years. Many new countries have followed this American model.

Democracy as a Structure of Government

Democracy as a form of government is based on clear rules. The first principle of a democratic government is the separation of powers to gain balance. The state power is divided:

The power of creating legislation rests with the ***Parliament***, whose members are elected by the people in fair and free elections. For instance, in our country, this function is performed by Congress, with its two chambers, the Senate and House of Representatives. In Great Britain, legislation is ruled by the British Parliament, with a Lower House (as well as the unelected Upper House); in Germany, the "parliament" is the Bundestag (as well as the Federal Council, which is not elected by the people); and in Switzerland, it is the Federal Assembly with the National Council and the Council of States (Senate). The task of a parliament is to pass laws which are binding and take effect across the country.

The ***Government*** of a country carries out the tasks assigned by the legislature. In the United States, this is the President with his Cabinet Secretaries. In Great Britain, the government is the Prime Minister with the Cabinet; in Germany, it is the Federal Chancellor with the Ministers; and in Switzerland, it is the Federal Council as a collective authority.

The laws passed by the parliament are reviewed by a ***Court*** to ensure that they are constitutional. Unclear circumstances, or disputes, are examined by the court to verify compliance with the laws passed. In the United States, the Supreme Court has the final authority to rule; in the United Kingdom it is the Supreme Court; and, in Germany, it is the Federal Constitutional Court.

Changes Caused by the French Revolution

The step from having all power concentrated in the hand of a monarch to the division of power was another milestone in human history. The most important and best-known change from monarchical power to separation of powers occurred in the French Revolution, in 1789.[5]

The French state had an institution, the Estates General (French: *États généraux*), which was created in 1302 and intended to represent all three classes: the clergy, the nobility, and the people. It was used to approve tax increases or sensitive treaties with foreign countries. It was also supposed to curtail the king's power somewhat, but its importance had declined more and more in the Age of Absolutism and, after 1614, the Estates were no longer convened.

As Louis XIV stated, "L'Etat c'est moi" ("I am the State"), which represented the peak of absolutist power around 1700. During the 18th century, France became heavily indebted due to its involvement in wars, especially in the Seven Years' War, as well as further excessive expenditures. Additional taxes were

5 Another process that also created a separation of powers happened in England by the English parliament during the 13th-17th centuries.

levied to reduce the king's debt burden, which further impoverished the masses.

Additionally, there were the ideas of the Enlightenment, of Montesquieu, Jean-Jacques Rousseau, John Locke, and other philosophers; in the monarchy's last years, paradoxically, French troops supported the insurgent colonies in North America—along with their democratic and republican ideals—against royal England. All of this, combined with crop failures in 1787 and 1788, exacerbated the contrasts between the absolutist regime and the masses of France's citizens.

The general crisis throughout the country forced the King to convene the Estates General again after 170 years. When he, supported by the nobility and clergy, did not recognize the third class, to which the citizens and peasants belonged, its representatives left the general assembly. In the ballroom at Royal Versailles Castle, they undertook with representatives of the other two classes to create the new National Assembly composed of all three classes.

The representatives in the Estate General also took the solemn oath not to terminate their Assembly until France had a constitution. When royal troops entered Paris, the people took up arms. The urban population rose against traditional governing and administrative organs, and the peasants' revolt opposed the feudal regime. With the storming of the Bastille prison on July 14, 1789, the revolution began.

At the conclusion of the revolution, the King was forced to accept a constitution, and a constitutional monarchy emerged. However, as resistance to the king grew within the country, as well as among the monarchies of Europe, the leading groups became increasingly radicalized, and in 1792, the monarchy was finally abolished in France. Louis XVI and his wife were executed.

In 1793/1794, the Jacobin Club ruled with dictatorial power and pushed through many innovations that are still in use today (standardization of weights and measures, a centralized bureaucracy, the abolition of all titles and privileges of the nobility and the churches, language standardization for laws, currency, markets, etc.). They also ruled, however, by utilizing terror.

The irony of history for France is that the period of a republic lasted ten years only, when Napoleon Bonaparte, a brilliant general in the 1790s, crowned himself Emperor of France in 1804. French history went on with another Empire and five different structures of republics from 1815 to present. Today, France is a functioning democracy in both structure and substance.

Basic Conditions for Democracy

For a democratic parliament to be elected, it is essential that citizens enjoy personal freedoms. Freedom of expression must be guaranteed, so everyone can justify and express their own opinions on any topic. Freedom of the press is also needed to disseminate these opinions. Freedom of assembly and religion are other rights of the people and people must have the right to found their own political parties.

Depending on the structures of the central authorities, the member states, districts, and municipalities are equipped with similar decision-making bodies. This creates a legal system that consistently includes the following values:

- The rights emanate from the people, who elect and thus determine their representatives. This is different from a Monarchy, where a King or an Emperor claims that his rights come from God.
- The elections must be carried out freely and fairly.

- The people participate in political processes and civic life as active citizens.
- The majority determines which laws are adopted.
- Government policies must reflect the wishes of the people.
- The rule of law is guaranteed, and the laws and procedures apply equally to all citizens.
- Government work must be done efficiently.

The Modern State

The structure of the separation of powers, the principles of the republic, and the guaranteed freedoms of citizens form the image of a modern state. Economic activities are derived from these freedoms: the free market economy. State activity thus becomes the regulating authority, the economy an acting authority. For a nation to operate successfully, these principles must be followed clearly.

The welfare of citizens and their protection is the responsibility of a democratic government. In other words, the legislators are responsible for orchestrating economic and political development that will secure safety and wellbeing, and a basic lifestyle for all citizens, including the needy. The primary reason we elect political officials is to manage the country and serve its citizens.

Democracy as a Political Program

Equality as a Principle

A democratic government offers the most balanced, authentic, and ideal form of ruling. It is a political program with noble goals.

One basic task of democracy is to guarantee social equality and the respect of the individual within a community. Democracy as principle is intended to protect all, including the less fortunate. The effort to create a balance between rich and poor, young and old, strong and weak, and between big and small must take precedence. Changes in favor of a democratic perspective are found in the cultivation of an ideology, which is responsible for how laws are framed. Laws must support equality. Laws must support the people. Laws must bring justice.

Alexis de Tocqueville and more:

"Therefore, the more thoroughly I examined the social condition of the free North Americans, the more clearly I saw the source in the equality of the estates, from which much else followed. I regard this situation as a point from which all my perceptions are explained."[6]

It is noticeable that "the equality of the estates" is cited as the "source" for the functioning of a democracy. It may be an

6 Alexis de Tocqueville, De la Démocratie en Amérique *(On Democracy in America)*, 1836

unfortunate choice of words, since it was the founding fathers' endeavor to abolish estates and to achieve equality among the citizens.

The goal of democracy is to create equality—it may be deduced that democracy first serves to fulfill simple basic needs such as food and housing. Today, at a higher level of economic development, the demands are different. A convergence of standards of living must be pursued to meet the vision set in the founding years of the United States.

The Economic Side of Democracy

Democracy is the political arm of a market economy in the capitalist world; it regulates the economy with legislation. The regulation of society is nothing new. The Code of Hammurabi, the oldest codification of society's rules, was created 3,700 years ago; its 282 laws regulated the everyday life of the Mesopotamian people.[7] In today's democratic society, laws are created not only for trade and taxes but also for education, health, security, environment, foreign policy, defense, and more.

Legislation sets the rules for fair pay, guarantees the fulfillment of contractual agreements and other obligations, protects the individual and the environment, and helps prepare for future infrastructure planning. Regulations limit economic activities for some people and unlock possibilities for others. Democracy, in

---

7 Hammurabi, the 6th Babylonian King, ruled from 1792 to 1750 B.C. The Code was discovered in 1901 by archaeologists in today's Iran. https://www.britannica.com/topic/Code-of-Hammurabi

this sense, offers the basic rules for living in society; it is a social construct to re-balance influence and power.

The coexistence of regulating production (*e.g.*, manufacturing goods) and providing (*e.g.*, goods and services) improves everyone's quality of life. Unless the power to regulate is abused, it protects the rich and the poor as well as large and small businesses. In the western world, the interaction between a democratic type of government and a market-based economy has been successful for a long time. It has enabled a majority of the population to live in dignity, with ample available food, housing, health, and culture. The laws of democracy apply to everyone. That is its recipe for success.

Part 2: The Constitution of the United States of America

The U.S. was Founded on Core Values and Democratic Principles

The story is compelling, even inspirational, for the founding of the United States was a milestone in human history. It is, for this reason, that we must begin with the 13 colonies (Delaware, Pennsylvania, Massachusetts Bay Colony [which included Maine], New Jersey, Georgia, Connecticut, Maryland, South Carolina, New Hampshire, Virginia, New York, North Carolina, and Rhode Island and Providence Plantations).

The first settlers were mostly English immigrants who struggled to reach the new land in the hope to find peace, independence and the right to determine their own destinies, to worship as they wished, and to live as they chose.

The Arrival of European Settlers

The discovery of the new continent in 1492 by Christopher Columbus and, in particular, the settlement of North America by Europeans, which began in 1607, meant that some countries in Europe could expand their territories within the next two centuries.

The area of today's United States consisted of territories that "belonged" to the kingdoms of England, France, and Spain. Many of these areas had been contested between England and France.

From 1754 to 1763, these disputes escalated into open warfare, namely, the French and Indian War, which was part of the so-called Seven Years' War in Europe. That war ended in 1763 with the Peace of Paris, and France losing all of its territories in North America.

This war with France had two principal effects on the relationship between the British settlers, on the new continent, and the English Crown. On one hand, the pressure of the Native Americans on the settlers was sufficiently diminished, so that the settlers felt safer to establish their new lives on this continent. On the other hand, the war had swallowed up an enormous amount of money, which the English King George III expected to recoup by imposing higher taxes and duties of all kinds on the settlers on the New Continent.

In principle, the settlers in North America were not against taxes; what they wanted was to be represented in the English parliament, so they could participate in the decision-making around their obligations. This, the King refused to grant. Instead, his Majesty repealed a number of laws made by the colonials, who more and more were moving toward self-government.

The King dissolved colonial parliaments, or hindered their work in other ways, through his loyalists enforcing his power. He was determined to limit self-determination in any respect, which then resulted in several confrontations.

The 1770 Boston Massacre was a confrontation of local people with British soldiers, with five deaths and several people injured. The Gaspee Affair of 1772 was an arson attack on a British ship in Rhode Island.

In his most destructive interventions, the King imposed high taxes on tea coming from Britain to the colonies, which led to the infamous "Boston Tea Party" in 1773. This political protest raised the spirit of the colonials, whose rallying cry was to change the relationship between the protagonists forever: "No Taxation without Representation", as it was used at the Stamp Action Congress of 1765, in New York.

The King responded with a blockade of the harbor and imposed more sanctions. Ultimately, his actions drove the colonials to resist and, eventually, abandon him and England.

After these Boston skirmishes, the other colonies lined up behind Massachusetts, even as most of them still held the intention of achieving a better relationship with the English Crown. Those who would come to be known as America's founding fathers created "organized resistance" to Britain; they met, in 1774, at the First Continental Congress in Philadelphia. Even though there were armed conflicts with the British troops, provincial congresses were formed in all 13 colonies. Together, they recruited a Continental Army, under the command of General George Washington.

A mere two years later, on July 2, 1776, a Second Continental Congress proclaimed the birth of the Free and Independent States, which initially formed a confederation. On July 4, 1776, the Declaration of Independence, written by one of the leading Virginia representatives, Thomas Jefferson, was adopted.[8]

---

[8] Prior to the Declaration of Independence of July 4, 1776, North Carolina and Virginia had the intention to separate from the British Crown and declared independence.

The Declaration of Independence of the United States of America

The Declaration of Independence expressed the belief that all men are created equal by God, and that they enjoy inalienable rights, which meant their rights could not be surrendered by them nor taken away from them: "We hold these truths to be self-evident; that all men are created equal, and they are endowed by their Creator with certain unalienable Rights; and among these are Life, Liberty, and the pursuit of Happiness".[9]

Even though all men were declared equal, the slaves were not given any rights. It was only after the Civil War was fought (1860–1865) that they would be acknowledged as having inalienable rights—in theory.

The Declaration (1) explained the reasons the colonies had to separate from Great Britain; (2) called for lawsuits against the King; and (3) explained that the colonies had to be free to protect their own rights. The purpose of the Declaration was to declare publicly as well as to all countries in Europe, that the new structure of government was based on the 20 principles stated therein.

[9] J. Rufus Fears, *"The Wisdom of History"*, Lecture 28: "Thomas Jefferson as Statesman" (Chantilly, VA: The Great Courses/The Teaching Company, 2007), p. 135

Reasons for Separation from the Crown

The separation from Great Britain was an act of national liberation by self-declaration. As noted, the People reserved for themselves the right to declare their independence, to be free, and to establish a new, free nation. They based their right to declare themselves free under the laws of God and nature.

These ideals were borrowed from the development of democracy in Athens in the 5th century B.C., when Socrates spoke of the law of God as applying to everyone (everyone in that period referred to men older than 30 years of age). Alexander the Great of Macedonia is often credited with saying that all people are equal and should be judged primarily on their virtue and character.[10] The Greek philosophers, especially the Stoics, taught that all men were equal under the goodness of a God as revealed in nature, and that everyone has life, freedom, and the pursuit of happiness as inalienable rights.

The Roman statesman, lawyer, and scholar, Marcus Tullius Cicero, declared, 100 years before Christ, that the law of nature was the law of God. It is a law that lies with God and lives every-

10 "Now that the wars are coming to an end, I wish you to prosper in peace. May all mortals from now on live like one people in concord and for mutual advancement. Consider the world as your country, with laws common to all and where the best will govern irrespective of tribe. I do not distinguish among men, as the narrow-minded do, both among Greeks and Barbarians. I am not interested in the descendants of the citizens or their racial origins. I classify them using one criterion: their virtue. For me every virtuous foreigner is a Greek and every evil Greek worse than a Barbarian. If differences ever develop between you never have recourse to arms but solve them peacefully. If necessary, I should be your arbitrator." While Alexander has been credited with having spoken these words, no source has ever been found, and there are doubts about the authorship of this statement.

where, and at all times. These laws were later subsumed into Christianity.

Another milestone in the development of democracy was the recognition of the Magna Carta Libertatum, in England in 1215, which states that everyone, including the King of England and his government, is subject to law. This document was actually drafted by the Archbishop of Canterbury and signed by King John of England and his barons, who did not trust the King. It insured that the rights of every individual would be guaranteed, and the right to justice and a fair trial would apply to all. Also, in England, a document called the "Bill of Rights", written in 1689, renewed the restrictions on the King and introduced democratic elections.

Finally, the English philosopher, John Locke (1632-1704), wrote that government was always set up by the people to protect the lives, freedom, and property of all citizens. Locke declared that, if a government cannot accomplish this task, revolution would not only be justified, it would become a duty of the people to undertake.

From all of the above points, "freedom" came to mean that everyone has the right to live as long as others are not harmed or damaged. Primarily, "damage" referred to the destruction and theft of property. The pursuit of happiness is equally protected, meaning that everyone is responsible for his or her own life, and not the state. As a German proverb says: Everyone is the smith of his luck. This ultimately boils down to the belief that freedom will make the world a better place for everyone (and, accordingly, losers must ascribe to themselves their own failures, which is the fundamental view in American society today).

Thomas Jefferson incorporated these thoughts on behalf of the 13 colonies in North America. His primary concern was that the new nation live and protect these ideals. The Declaration of Independence introduced a radical new idea of an individual as a citizen: you declare yourself a citizen on the basis of natural law. This is a big difference from the view of the royal houses of that time in Europe, who attributed their power to God ("ruler of God's grace"). The subjects (not "citizens" in the sense of "citizens" as we think of them) had to submit to this hierarchy; they were not independent entities of any kind.

The Constitution

The United States Constitution begins with these famous words: "We the People of the United States, in order to form a more perfect Union, establish Justice, insure domestic Tranquility, provide for the common defense, promote the general Welfare, and secure the Blessings of Liberty to ourselves and our Posterity, do ordain and establish this Constitution for the United States of America". The text was predominately designed by James Madison and was signed by a majority—39—of the delegates at the Constituent Assembly in Philadelphia on September 17, 1787. The Constitution came into force on March 4, 1789, after the parliaments of nine of the 13 former colonies approved the text.

Madison's concern was for the ongoing protection of the citizens of the United States, of their natural right to life, freedom, and the pursuit of happiness through the government. It expressed the fundamental rights of the nation's citizens and bound the government to protect those rights in every area of the nation's life.

The government, as designed in the Constitution, rests on three pillars: inherent rights, government by the people, and a separation of powers. Self-government is the core idea of the

Constitution, and the basic structure explicitly defines the American government system.

It divides the government into three powers: the legislative authority (Congress) which enacts the laws; the Executive (President) who executes the laws; and the judicial branch (the Courts) which both interpret the law when it is challenged and, in the event of a dispute between two or more parties, interpret the specific meaning of the laws as applicable to this dispute.

The Constitution clearly articulates the legitimacy, structures, and responsibilities of the three arms of Government: legislature, executive, and judicial. The document brings forth a balance and distribution of power between these three bodies, known as "checks and balances". For example, laws are passed by the government that are approved by the majority of members of Congress and the President on behalf of the people. Before a bill can become law, it must be adopted by both Chambers of Congress (see two chambers of Congress, below) and then signed by the President. Once the bill becomes law, the Executive—the President—is bound to follow it, and the Judiciary is the final arbiter of interpreting it. None of these three authorities rules alone. The Constitution further regulates the responsibilities of the central government and the member states in relation to one another.

From the beginning of the new country, the legislature—Congress—was divided into two chambers. Every state is represented by two Senators in the Senate chamber, regardless of its size and number of resident citizens. In the House of Representatives, the number of residents in a state determines how many Representatives will be sent to the House chamber from that state.

Thus, the tasks and duties of the government are specified in the Constitution: The government is the mediator, guarantor, and protector of the freedoms; justification comes from the approval of the governed, and no longer from God. The government has a limited right to intervene in the lives of individuals. If the government does not achieve the stated goals, the governed have the right to change or remove the government and appoint new leaders (John Locke).

The creations of the Declaration of Independence and the Constitution resulted in the United States becoming the first nation in the world to articulate and adopt these principles from the onset. Those who recognize and live by these principles can become citizens of the new country. In comparison, in most countries, citizenship is only obtained through birth, *i.e.,* via the parents (*ius sanguinis*). In the United States, one automatically becomes a citizen if born in the country (*ius solis*), even if their mother was only passing through.

The Bill of Rights

Although one might deduce that, between the Constitution and the Declaration of Independence, all the rights to which citizens would be entitled had been articulated and were well-protected, James Madison soon realized that certain "human rights" had actually been overlooked. He soon had to address criticism from the parliaments of the founding states, that certain human rights were mentioned insufficiently or not at all in the document.

On June 12, 1789, Madison acted in response to the criticisms against the young government by presenting a list of 12 amendments, stating important rights of citizens *as* citizens and against their own government. The first ten of these additions came to be known as The Bill of Rights, a veritable fundamental rights catalog.

The English "Magna Carta Libertatum" of 1215, the English Bill of Rights of 1689, as well as the Virginia Declaration of Rights of 1776 served as the model for the American Bill of Rights, which named the specific protective measures the government would guarantee for the benefit of its citizens. Thus, for the first time in the history of mankind, it would be clearly and unequivocally stated that all citizens are equal under the law and subject to the laws of the country. These rights were protected from violations by civil servants—that is, government agents—and private individuals as well. In short, The Bill of Rights guarantees the civil rights set forth in it, and freedoms to every individual citizen.

Human rights arise from being human

Human rights are moral principles and norms of human behavior. They are inalienable rights that naturally belong to each person. They apply to everyone and at any time, and they are the same for everyone, regardless of language, age, ethnicity, religion, and other criteria.

Constitutional Law: Legal basis of a state or groupings of states

Constitutional rights are all the rights that the constitution of any nation, state, or organization grants to its citizens. Constitutional rights are laws to be upheld by the governing body that created them.

Civil rights: relationship between citizens and the state

Civil rights, as compared to constitutional rights, are guidelines and ideas of what citizens should have and become the laws of the country. Civil rights typically are the rights of individuals to live free from oppression and discrimination, to vote, to take advantage of public education, the right to a fair trial, the right to government services, and the right to use public facilities.

Civil rights are the legal rights that protect individuals from discrimination.

Civil rights arise from a legal grant, such as the rights granted to American citizens by the United States Constitution.

Liberties: Part of fundamental rights that protect citizens from the state

Civil liberties are freedoms that are guaranteed by the Constitution to protect against tyranny. Citizens' rights include freedom of religion, speech, and press; freedom of assembly; freedom to petition the government; the right to use arms; the right to a fair trial; and the prohibition of cruel and unusual punishments.

The Imperfect and Flawed Human Being—Laws Create Order—The Need for Governance

Why are there laws? Why does everyone have to observe the same rules when driving a car, to comply with the obligation to file a tax return, or to pay for a desired product before they can be said to own it? If you follow the laws, you should generally expect to live a peaceful life. If, on the other hand, you are of the opinion that these laws do not apply to you, you should generally expect a different reaction: warnings, fines, even imprisonment. So, what justifies the variety of laws we have to obey?

It is common for humans to live in smaller and larger communities over the course of their lives. The movement begins at birth and expands to include families and social groups, communities, regions, even other countries.

The character of a person is diverse, if not imperfect. It has remained unchanged for centuries.[11] Love, hate, loyalty, greed, hunger for power, forbearance, commitment, arrogance, insecurity, honesty, pride, contempt—these are common traits that may or may not guarantee a peaceful or a successful society.

Living in communities is natural for human beings. Values such as consciousness, ethics, honesty, kindness, responsibility, and integrity become important. Laws are guidelines and help protect people.

The interaction of laws and traits can be divided into "hardware" and "software" or structure and substance. On the one hand, regulations and laws are clearly established and reinforced, like the separation of powers of a state, the structure of state authorities, and the rights and obligations of citizens.

On the other hand—the "software" or substance—the way of thinking, speaking, and acting shapes the democracy. How can we, as a society, live and function peacefully and flourish? Respect for all citizens, the individual as well as groups, honesty, order, and loyalty are requirements.

---

11 J. Rufus Fears, *ante.*

Rules, regulations, and laws must serve the life of the individual and the community. The majority and the minority will meet and find a compromise, which is democratic.

Democracy offers the structure for a diversity of people with different opinions, needs, and goals. Democracy, as a form of rule and government, collects a wide variety of opinions, and, then through compromise, translates those diverse views into uniform regulations. Thus, it can be said that a democratic government is an institution of compromise and problem-solving for effective, efficient, and ethical solutions for living.

> "I would unite with anybody to do right and with nobody to do wrong."
>
> Frederick Douglass

Part 3: Democratic Principles

After evaluating the theory of democracy, let us have a look at the practical side. We use elections and the understanding of democracy as our criteria for comparing the requirements of the Constitution with everyday political life. The keywords, "voter discrimination" and "gerrymandering", are used to refer to topics that have been the conversation for a long time, are highly controversial, and may even seem boring to some readers. Concrete examples—more specifically regarding the 2016 and 2018 elections—are presented in **Appendix 1**, where interested readers can find relevant details. Below, I expound on the lessons learned from such incidents.

Democratic Principles—Voting Rights

On Tuesday after the first Monday of November of each election year, American citizens are invited to elect the members of the two chambers of Congress, namely, all of the 435 Representatives and one third of the 100 Senators. Since the United States has no mandatory registration for residences, voters are required to register in advance in their respective states to vote in the elections. Of course, an entry in the voters' registry is only possible if an official ID is presented. The Constitution makes it the responsibility of the states to organize and hold their own elections.

The rule is and has always been: one person, one vote. Initially, voting rights were limited to men of a certain age and property owners. In theory, every American citizen has the right to vote.

We know that a number of unethical restrictions severely reduce the actual number of eligible voters. In 2016, the U.S. Census Bureau estimated that one seventh of the electorate were unable to vote.[12] Here below is a list of actual issues:[13]

- Problems with voter registration
- Inaccurate election list clean-up
- Strict requirements for voter ID cards and ballot papers
- Voter confusion due to administrative errors and misinformation
- Voter intimidation and harassment
- Poll closures and long lines
- Malfunctioning voting equipment
- Disenfranchisement of people involved in prior criminal actions

Voter Restrictions

The list of often minor restrictions on voting rights from 2016 and 2018 is alarmingly long. Restrictions preventing voters from casting their ballots were reported in 21 of the 50 states. The

---

12 U.S. Census Bureau, "Voting and Registration in the Election of November 2016", available at https://www.census.gov/data/tables/time-series/demo/voting-and-registration/p20-580.html

13 Danielle Root and Adam Barclay, Voter Suppression During the 2018 Midterm Elections, *American Progress*, November 18, 2018, at https://www.americanprogress.org/issues/democracy/reports/2018/11/20/461296/voter-suppression-2018-midterm-elections/

details are described in **Appendix 1**. Many states are mentioned several times.

The frequent changes or adaptations of the electoral laws raise questions of whether the electoral laws in force have not been able to cope with the problems mentioned above. Can we argue that hidden motives or malicious intentions are the reason for the constant changes in the electoral laws?

Ideally, electoral laws should be structured such that all eligible voters have easy access to the ballot boxes, both in terms of time and location. The goal of democratic elections is to achieve high voter turnout. This enhances the legitimacy of those who get elected.

It may seem petty to mention minor imperfections such as broken voting machines or poorly accessible voting stations. As large numbers of such irregularities have an impact on the final voting result, one could argue that they are fraudulent.

If 21 states introduce or maintain such barriers in one or more ways, then one can consider it a nationwide problem for democracy. Tolerating malfunctioning voting machines, purging voting lists, restricting open hours, moving polling stations locally, closing-down polling stations altogether, or unprepared election workers is negligent or could be abuse of power. It clearly indicates a broad problem. Limiting the eligibility or number of certain voters in order to influence election results by means of small-scale harassment is equally repugnant. It is a deceit on the voter.

What is the real reason for so many voting restrictions? The two major parties are doing their utmost to win voters over to their side. One of the two parties tries to keep voter turnout low because this improves its results, whereas the other tries to increase voter turnout, because high turnout benefits that party.

The Organization of Elections

In order to get to the bottom of this question, we have to examine closely how elections are organized. The Constitution entrusts the state governments in Section 4 with implementing the elections both for Congress and for their own States' governance.

Like the Federal government in Washington, each state government is usually dominated by one of the two major parties. The elections and all preparatory work are organized by the Secretaries of State of the respective state governments. Since one of the two major parties normally controls the State, it is this party that performs this task. In other words, a party organizes its own elections! Obviously, and due to basic human nature, a party will accordingly be able to influence the preparation for the election and thereby enhance its own chances of prevailing.

While every state can opt to create an Independent Election Commission, very few states have them. At this writing, the only independent commissions are in Florida, Hawaii, Illinois, Maryland, New York, North Carolina, Oklahoma, South Carolina, Virginia, and Wisconsin.[14]

Everywhere else, parties follow their own objectives and are not always concerned with correct and democratic processes. The extent to which restrictions have been applied throughout the country, however, can only be explained by partisan interest and not by any real attempts to fight voter fraud or serve voters generally. Still, voter fraud is generally a small problem.

The clause in the Constitution stipulating that the states are responsible for organizing their own elections may be one

14 National Conference of State Legislatures (NCSL), Election Administration at the State Level, https://www.ncsl.org/research/elections-and-campaigns/election-administration-at-state-and-local-levels.aspx

constitutional error with the most dangerous consequences for democracy.

Voting Rights as a Test for Democratic Thinking

The *Federal Election Commission* (FEC), in particular, should play a leading role in the nation's voting process. *Should,* however, is a far cry from *does.* Reality paints a different picture. Ignoring FEC's concerns is the result of years of unilateral interference by the Republican party. "The leader of the Republican Senate Majority, Senator McConnell, is really the whole key to the FEC", wrote Andy Kroll in a 2011 piece for *Mother Jones*. "He realized several years ago that a very effective way to minimize the effect of Federal laws is to undermine the regulator".[15]

Unfortunately, a proposal to launch a National Voter Registration Day has been rejected by mostly Republican circles, because they suspect it will benefit Democrats.[16] It is striking to see that many states with Republican governors refuse to consider different registration times and places, such as on Sundays in front of churches. Communities and states, mainly in southern states, have practically denied citizens the right to vote, since these citizens do not have the time or means of transport to show up at the timeslots and places decreed by the law. Civil rights activists have repeatedly decried this practice as undemocratic.

The Civil War (1860-1865) ended slavery in the South (*see more below*), and the affected Black Americans became full citizens of the United States. However, the southern states of the

---

15 Andy Kroll, "What the FEC?" *Mother Jones,* April 18, 2011, quoted in Mann/Ornstein, *ante,* p. 154

16 *Ibid.*, p. 136

defeated Confederate States of America found ways to deny voting rights to the new citizens by using various arguments. The *Jim Crow Laws* (named after a theatrical protagonist who portrayed the character of Blacks from the viewpoint of Whites) stipulated writing and reading tests, election fees, property ownership requirements, character tests, and proof that the applicant's grandfather was entitled to vote, among other things, as prerequisites for granting the right to vote.

The denial of voting rights to Black Americans went on for 100 years, in which there were numerous protests and demonstrations calling for the implementation of voting rights reforms. The Civil Rights Movement of the 1950s and 1960s—with representatives such as Martin Luther King, Jr., and Malcolm X—increased public pressure.

In 1965, in response to the Civil Rights Movement from 1954-1968, President Lyndon B. Johnson signed the Voting Rights Act into law to guarantee voting rights for all American citizens, and to eliminate voter discrimination based on race. The Act was designed to strengthen the 14th Amendment (which grants citizenship to anyone "born or naturalized in the United States") and the 15th Amendment ("...the right of citizens of the United States to vote shall not be denied or abridged by the United States or by any State on account of race, color, or previous condition of servitude."). It was an effort to insist upon citizens' rights, regardless of race, language, or creed. It outlawed the discriminatory voting practices adopted in many southern states after the Civil War.

Improvements and Setbacks

The Constitution of the United States of America grants each state full discretion to determine voter qualifications for its residents.

With the Voting Rights Act of 1965, however, regulations and restrictions on the states' freedom to discriminate were made at the Federal level. The law stipulates that state and community regulations must not infringe upon Federal election principles. Changes affecting Federal guarantees require the approval of the U.S. Attorney General, or the U.S. District Court for the District of Columbia, to ensure that the intended new laws do not discriminate against protected minorities.

The introduction of the Voting Rights Act of 1965 led to a steady increase in the number of voters. The provisions for the protection of minorities were set to expire after a certain period of time and were repeatedly extended from 1975 onward. In 2006, Shelby County in Alabama filed a lawsuit against the Federal government's claim to determine voting rights, arguing that circumstances 30 years prior to the election were no longer applicable. The Supreme Court ruled in favor of the County (Shelby County vs. Holder, 2006).

As a result of this ruling, about 1,000 polling stations were closed in several southern states, and also in Ohio and Wisconsin, primarily in areas with a majority of Black residents.[17] Regulations familiar from the past were re-introduced, such as restrictions on early voting, voter list clean-ups, and the imposition of strict voter identification rules.[18]

Author Ari Berman points out that, between 2011 and 2015 in 49 states, nearly 400 voting restrictions were introduced.[19] This resulted in an average of eight new restrictions per state. The restrictions were peddled as measures to curtail voter fraud. *New York Times* reporter Brendan Nyhan explains that voter

---

17 *"Polling Place Politics", www.pewtrusts.org. Retrieved 2018-09-05*

18 *Ibid.*

19 Ari Berman, *Give Us the Ballot. The Modern Struggle for Voting Rights in America* (New York: Farrar, Straus and Giroux, 2015)

fraud, as such, is rare. The myth, however, is widespread.[20] Voter fraud in America is frequently debated in the media and courts, where actual cases of unauthorized voter registrations are generally proven case by case.

Conclusion:

Remember, "We hold these truths to be self-evident; that all men are created equal, and they are endowed by their Creator with certain unalienable Rights...." Voting rights are still controversial and are interpreted in a limiting and disadvantageous way.

The leap from the theoretical model of the right to vote to the picture of the voting reality is strikingly large. It is easy to postulate ideal guidelines. Implementing the formal and substantive ideas of democracy is a demanding challenge.

It is unacceptable that electoral workers at all levels across the country do not know the simplest and most important rules of democracy, or consciously ignore them. Politicians such as Secretaries of States, with their legal staffs, are involved in the restriction of voters—yes, they determine the restrictions. Pestering voters to show an ID and possibly making disrespectful remarks, including threats, at the polls, are anti-democratic and vicious.

An election list clean-up needs to be performed by unbiased personnel, committed to a democratic outcome. It is unacceptable to have voting machines in operation that are malfunctioning or purposely disabled. It takes ethical and impartial leadership to

20 Brendan Nyhan, "Voter Fraud is Rare, but Myth is Widespread", *The New York Times,* June 10, 2014

manage the voting process! The *substantive values* of democracy are not being lived.

It is necessary to get to know the values of democracy exactly, to train all people involved in the voting process and to apply the democratic rules in everyday political life. Only a broad consensus in substantive ideas about democracy can soften the loosening of the deadlocked fronts and clear the way for fair elections.

Democratic Principles—Ethical Elections

Assessment of the 2018 Governor's Election in Georgia

The nomination of Georgia's Secretary of State, Brian Kemp, as a candidate for the position of governor was immediately followed by criticisms and calls for him to resign and to resolve the obvious conflict of interest. Former President Jimmy Carter and several interest groups (Common Cause—a civil organization for free and fair elections, and NAACP—a multiracial civil rights movement) pointed out this conflict of interest. Kemp totally ignored these complaints and there was no further resistance. Kemp was elected with a majority of 53,000 votes. Georgia has a population of 10.62 million.

Here is the reality. When the votes were recounted to prove the candidate's majority, as many as 50,000 votes were rejected as "unapproved" and 3,000 others were withheld. Unapproved voter registrations? The decision of approval or non-approval of registration was made by the Secretary of State of Georgia, who was Brian Kemp, the candidate. In any case, the voting results and the results of the investigation show that the election's outcome was not only very close, but probably a mere coincidence, and maybe even falsified.

Those who can organize and influence their own election are in a blatant conflict of interest. Those who do not recognize this are lacking knowledge of the substance of democracy. In addition, to an external observer, this demonstrates clearly that dubious methods, which are obviously not democratic, are being used.

The 2018 gubernatorial election in Georgia illustrates that, in the cradle of modern democracy, power politics is stronger today than honest considerations for a fair democratic election. The inability to learn and live in accordance with democratic values is a recurring theme in American politics.

As a consequence, the country has become extremely divided in recent years. The political actors have proven incapable of governing the country with democratic values and instruments. Selfish interests and the wellbeing of the country are not kept separate.

This potential conflict of interest would have been easy to fix—namely by assigning the responsibility for approving or disapproving the candidate's election to an independent commission, and the same could be done in all states.

Democratic Principles—200 Years of Gerrymandering?

Even in the early history of the young country, as evidenced by the *Gerry-Mander* example from 1812[21], the right to redraw voting districts was not understood as a tool to promote democracy and equality, or to ensure a fair representation of the electorate, but rather as a way to satisfy personal or party interests.

Section 4 of the Constitution clearly states that state legislators and governors have the right and duty to organize Federal elections. That includes the right to define congressional districts. Just a few states have Independent Redistricting Commissions whose impartial authority guarantees a fair election process. These states are Alaska, Arizona, California, Colorado, Hawaii, Idaho, Michigan, Missouri, Montana, and Washington State.[22]

Gerrymandering, or "manipulating electoral district boundaries", is facilitated by the requirement to re-adjust the voting districts every ten years, based on the results of the national census. This will be the case once again in 2020. The purpose is to adjust the number of Representatives based on the population changes in the respective states. In terms of the allocation of seats to the states, the applicable regulations stipulate that approximately the same number of individuals in each of the states should be represented by one Representative in Congress. Seven states have only one Representative each in the House of Representatives because

21 Named for Governor Elbridge Gerry of Massachusetts and the form of a salamander, from the shape of a new voting district on a map drawn when Gerry was in office (1812). The creation of the new district was felt to favor Gerry's party, and, when the map (with claws, wings, and fangs added) was published in the Boston *Weekly Messenger*, it was titled *The Gerry-Mander.*

22 https://ballotpedia.org/Independent_redistricting_commissions

they have very few residents. The minimum is one Representative per state, and this cannot be changed.

The Supreme Court's Discussion in 2019

Gerrymandering has been a controversial subject for decades because the potential injustices in drawing election boundaries are obviously undemocratic. Thus, the Supreme Court has been called upon, on several occasions, to correct the distorted representation in the House of Representatives. The last time was in June 2019.

In the cases Common Cause v. Rucho and Lamone v. Benisek, the Supreme Court decided in 2019 that it was not its job to intervene in what is the responsibility of political and state legislative bodies, and thus left this task to the governments and legislatures of the states. The Supreme Court's decision in June 2019 is materially correct because, under the Constitution, it is the political authorities who are to create and change laws, not the courts. In this respect, the Court's decision indicates a clear commitment to the separation of powers.

Chief Justice Roberts, who wrote the decision for the Court, did not say the current system of drawing districts is desirable as a matter of policy. "Excessive partisanship in districting leads to results that reasonably seem unjust", he wrote. "The districting plans at issue here are highly partisan, by any measure. The question is whether the courts below appropriately exercised judicial power when they found them unconstitutional as well".[23]

The answer, Roberts wrote, is no, as courts lack the authority and competence to decide when politics has played too large a

[23] The Editorial Board, "Politicians Can Pick Their Voters, Thanks To The Supreme Court", *The New York Times,* June 27, 2019

role in redistricting. "There are no legal standards discernible in the Constitution for making such judgments", the Chief Justice wrote,[24] "let alone limited and precise standards that are clear, manageable and politically neutral." Roberts noted that his majority opinion was a modest one that recognized the limits of judicial power. "No one can accuse this court of having a crabbed view of the reach of its competence", he wrote. "But we have no commission to allocate political power and influence in the absence of a constitutional directive or legal standards to guide us in the exercise of such authority".[25]

"Federal judges have no license to reallocate political power between the two major political parties, with no plausible grant of authority in the Constitution, and no legal standards to limit and direct their decisions", Roberts wrote.[26] The Supreme Court stipulated that the 200 years' old problem of Gerrymandering has to be resolved at the state level.

Perhaps a more liberal Justice would have interpreted his or her responsibility as taking account of the fact that a part of the electorate, in this instance, was being granted a higher proportion of the seats than it was entitled to, based on the number of votes cast. Certainly, Justice Kagan would have been one such Justice.

As the spokeswoman for the minority in the Court, Elena Kagan expressed her opinion clearly about this ruling: "The practices challenged in these cases imperil our system of government... Part of the court's role in that system is to defend its foundations. None is more important than free and fair elections."[27]

---

24 *Ibid.*

25 *Ibid.*

26 Jess Bravin and Brent Kendall, "Supreme Court Declines to Set Limits on Political Gerrymandering", *The Wall Street Journal*, June 27, 2019

27 The Editorial Board, *ante*

The repeated redrawing of voting districts with the intention of giving one party an advantage is quite clearly not democratic. It is shameful that gerrymandering has been practiced in the United States for over 200 years. It represents a distortion of the voters' will, and infringes on one of the most important fundamental rights in a democratic country.

Gerrymandering Is Intolerable—Gerrymandering Is an Issue

Gerrymandering makes fair elections impossible. Gerrymandering is large-scale election fraud. However, the fact that the organization of elections is entrusted to the states enables this egregious distortion of the voting process to continue. With the imprimatur of the Highest Court in the land, it will remain legal for the legislature of any state which is controlled by one party to approve the redrawing of electoral district boundaries as it sees fit. And that is true, at least, unless and until this matter comes again before a Supreme Court with a more committed spirit of democracy.

Ironically, the fact that the states are responsible for organizing elections reinforces the point of criticism that these authorities determine their own competencies. It cannot be assumed that these bodies would be willing to hand over their power to an independent election commission, for example.

Opinion polls show that voter restrictions and gerrymandering are clearly rejected by both Democratic and Republican voters.[28] The reader's columns of *The New York Times* referred to the latest ruling from June 2019 with the expression, "a black day for

28 Jess Bravin and Brent Kendall, *ante*

American democracy". It also stated that gerrymandering was at a "banana-republic level".[29]

On the other hand, letters to the editor of *The Wall Street Journal* approved of this ruling to the extent it assured state control of the process, albeit with the wish that changes should be made quickly through the introduction of legislation by the states.[30]

As noted earlier, gerrymandering machinations have been practiced for over 200 years. There have been repeated attempts to correct this influence on elections. For example, on the first day of the 116th Congress (January 3, 2019), the House of Representatives adopted a bill named the *For The People Act of 2019,* introduced by Representative John Sarbanes (D, Maryland), with requirements relating to voting rights, campaign financing, and government ethics. In order for the bill to become law, the Senate also had to ratify it. However, Republican Senate majority leader Mitch McConnell clearly declared that the bill was "not going to go anywhere in the Senate",[31] thereby killing it.

Details to Attachment 2: I created a list with the seat distribution of the House of Representatives according to the proportional electoral system. The seat distribution corresponds roughly to the percentage of voters. Please see the overview to 50 U.S. states here, below or on the webpage

www.restore-our-democracy.com/

29 The Editorial Board, *ante*

30 Bravin and Kendall, *ante*

31 Jamil Smith, "Mitch McConnell, Enemy of the Vote", *RollingStone,* January 31, 2019

The districts created through gerrymandering often have strange geographic shapes. Some of the ridiculous assignments of regions resulted in fascinating titles like, The Praying Mantis (a Maryland district), Goofy Kicking Donald Duck (in Pennsylvania), or The Upside-down Elephant (a district in Texas). This only further exemplifies what a mockery of democracy this practice of line drawings has become.[32]

America's Most Gerrymandered Congressional Districts

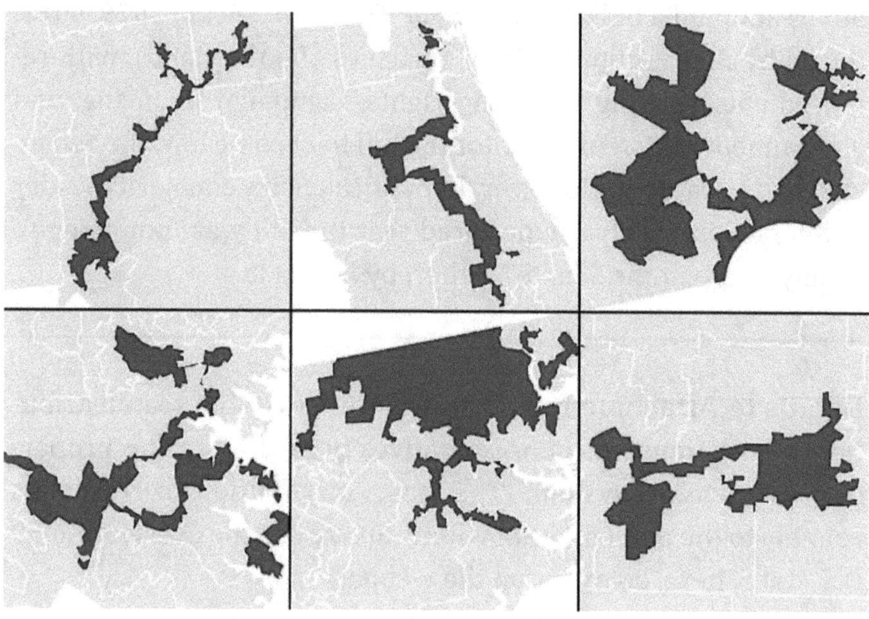

[32] Christopher Ingraham, "America's most gerrymandered districts", *The Washington Post,* May 15, 2014

Conclusion:

Gerrymandering is a legal voter fraud: a minority of voters gets a majority of seats. This is the result of a covert provision in the Constitution to allow the state legislator to manipulate the voting results legally. It is clearly stated in the Constitution's Section 4, that the individual states decide on how the voting districts will be drawn.

Most Americans demand the elimination of the partisan Gerrymandering. It has now become urgent that the 50 states implement laws guiding their state authorities to draw the boundaries of the voting districts independently of partisan interests.

A Monarch in North Carolina

The following was taken from an article that appeared in *The New York Times*, "Supreme Court Bars Challenges to Partisan Gerrymandering":

> "One case decided in a court in North Carolina concerned a plan drawn by Republican state lawmakers in 2016 that included a criterion called, "partisan advantage."
>
> The state's congressional delegation, in a purple state *(i.e., a mixed party state)* in which neither party had a distinct edge, was at the time made up of 10 Republicans and three Democrats. A key goal, lawmakers said, was "to maintain the current partisan makeup of North Carolina's congressional delegation."
>
> "I think electing Republicans is better than electing Democrats," explained David Lewis, a Republican member

> of the General Assembly's redistricting committee, Co-Chair of the Elections committee, responsible for the voter identification legislation as well as his work on the most recent round of redistricting in the State of North Carolina. "So, I drew this map to help foster what I think is better for the country."
>
> "I propose that we draw the maps to give a partisan advantage to 10 Republicans and three Democrats," he said, "because I do not believe it's possible to draw a map with 11 Republicans and two Democrats."

The plan worked. In 2016, Republican congressional candidates won 53 percent of the statewide vote. But, as predicted, they again won in 10 of the 13 congressional districts, or 77 percent of them.[33] According to a fair representation, the 47% votes for Democrats should get 6 seats while the 53% votes for Republicans would have 7 seats (see Appendix 2). David Lewis forced the outcome of this election abusing his power, clearly an unfair distribution of seats by Gerrymandering.

Conclusion

We lack the knowledge of *substance* of democracy, the theory of democracy. The values of democracy are the source of democratic rules. It is the thinking of democracy, the ideas and values which constitute a democracy. Democratic thinking is essential for guaranteeing correct elections. Having correct elections is a long process. Democratic principles must be observed and applied at every step of the way.

33 Adam Liptak, "Supreme Court Bars Challenges to Partisan Gerrymandering," *The New York Times*, June 27, 2019.

Learning about substantive democracy is a process and requires compassion. Open your ears, listen, and pay attention to what Americans with different values need and want.

Democratic Principles—The Role of the Parties

Candidate Selection for Political Positions

Anyone wishing to be elected to a political position in the United States has a simple way to announce their candidacy. All they will have to do is pick up a microphone and announce their intention. In most states, a number of signatures of voters is required to get on the ballot. However, they must also have sufficient funds behind them and must be able to gather a staff of advisors to handle the details of all aspects related to their campaign.

A promising candidacy must be able to raise a lot of money. First and foremost, television advertising is expensive, but an organization that will distribute election posters and write election documents also requires a great deal of effort and expense. This is the reason why candidates tend to seek followers who will contributes funds to the candidate's campaign, including various individuals, businesses, and other groups. It is true that there are small donors whose actions prove their support for the goals and values for which the candidate stands; they will cast their ballots for this candidate. Far more important, however, are wealthy opinion-makers and influential groups who also donate.

Affluent supporters rarely act out of idealism; rather, they are motivated by having their personal interests addressed, which largely explains the character of American politics today: They expect their candidates to defend their interests.[34] A thin line is soon crossed, and a successful candidate becomes directly dependent on these donors. Once elected, they are expected to repay the favor. This makes legislators very receptive to the use of undemocratic means.

Party Discipline: "I'd Rather Be a Russian Than a Democrat"

These words were printed on two t-shirts that were seen at an election event of the Republican Party in Ohio on August 5, 2018.[35] Since then, the t-shirts with these slogans have become available for sale on Amazon.

One can only ask: Are the two t-shirt wearers not American citizens? Are they so committed to their party that they have forgotten the fact that they are Americans? This slogan caused a passing stir in the area and in the press, but the statement, as such, is terrifying.

It can hardly be assumed that wearers of such t-shirts plan on moving to the utopian land of Russia any time soon. But it is much more important to ask why there is such an intense hatred of the other party, and what happened to democracy in the process? Is it their own insecurity that causes them to cling to this negative image? Jonathan Ladd refers to this frame of mind as

34 Peter Mathews, *Dollar Democracy: With Liberty and Justice for Some* (Amazon, 2014), pp. 1-10

35 Zack Beauchamp, "Trump's Republican Party, explained in one photo", *Vox*, Aug. 6, 2018

"negative partnership": You don't vote for one party because you love it, but rather because you completely reject the other party or its candidates: "They'd rather have a Republican in office, however unorthodox and unqualified, than any kind of Democrat."[36] Ladd explains this is one of the most important phenomena of our time.

Why should the rejection of the other party be expressed with such defensive reflexes? The strong attachment to a party resembles an affiliation with a church or a religious order. And: "Many Republicans voted for their party's nominee primarily in order to avoid a Clinton presidency."[37]

These indicate a lack of action in favor of the country's well-being. Politicians are on a troubled, self-fulfilling path to accommodate the wealthy. Party lines are placed ahead of the country's welfare and its many problems. In many states, access to voting by many voters is blocked, and the will of voters can be grossly distorted, if not falsified. Election procedures in 39 states are not regulated democratically.

Party Membership and the Contempt for Different Political Conviction

The animosity between the Democratic party and the Republican party is embarrassing. Party members are extremely hostile to the opposing party's members. Contempt is the underlining motive. Leadership is missing.

Given the entrenched party lines, a diversity of opinions is no longer discernible. Whoever dares to disagree with their party's

---

36 Jonathan Ladd, "Negative Partisanship may be the most toxic form of polarization", *Vox*, June 2, 2017

37 *Ibid.*

statements becomes an opponent, even an enemy. A peculiar kind of loyalty is demanded. In a real democracy, people with different opinions would not be seen as opponents, let alone enemies, but, rather, as fellow citizens, as other Americans who are entitled to participate in the democratic process.

What is remarkable is that up until about 1990, there were Senators and Representatives who determined the country's political direction through compromises. How was it possible that sentiments among legislators changed so dramatically into this friend or foe picture?

Former Congressman and Speaker of the House, Newt Gingrich, has been and remains a key player in polarizing the two parties.[38] As Mann and Ornstein state: "Gingrich deserves a dubious kind of credit for many of the elements that have produced the current state of politics".[39] In their chapter, "Seeds of Dysfunction", the authors list several reasons for the current gridlock in government.[40]

Commitment to the party line by party members and members of Congress has had repercussions on the composition of voters since the 1970s. Mann and Ornstein wrote that emphasis on party interests resulted in voters becoming more loyal to the party than to the country—something that parallels the party members' behavior.[41] This is true of both major parties. The aggressive, non-compromising atmosphere within Congress since the 1980s has politically polarized the United States.

---

38 Newt L. Gingrich was a member of the House of Representatives from 1979 to 1999, and Speaker of the House from 1995 to 1999.

39 Thomas E. Mann and Norman J. Ornstein, *It's Even Worse Than it Looks: How the American Constitutional System Collided with the New Politics of Extremism* (New York: Basic Books, 2012), p. 42

40 *Ibid.*, p. 31

41 *Ibid.*, p. 101

"The pathologies we've identified, old and new, provide incontrovertible evidence of people who have become more loyal to party than to country".[42] In other words, the party's ideology has become more important than the country's welfare. Any desired outcome must favor the party, regardless of whether or not it is positive for the country. The main concern of politicians is to be in control and have the power to govern mainstream opinion. To assert that you are right, even though you may have distorted the facts, is now simply politics as usual.

Party loyalty is as strong as it was in the former sphere of influence of the Communist parties of the Soviet Union and its Eastern European vassal states until 1989, with one important distinction. Party membership in the United States is sought voluntarily; in the Soviet Empire, it was an avowal of belief and a way to enter the circle of power.

The Public Appearance of Senators and Representatives

Party politics have become bickering performances on television's grand stage. In his memoir, *Duty: Memoirs of a Secretary at War*, Robert Gates wrote that members of Congress immediately change their opinions when a television camera shows up.[43] Their social behavior turns from understanding and conciliatory to crude and uncivilized as they put their own interests before the needs of the country. Their activities appear focused on their own re-elections, and the favorable response of a public opinion poll seems to be of utmost importance.

---

42 *Ibid.*

43 Robert M. Gates, *Duty: Memoirs of a Secretary at War* (New York: Borzoi Book/Alfred Knopf Publishing, 2014), p. 387

That is what it is all about: self-preservation through re-election. This is so important to them that the average congressperson spends more time fundraising than he or she does working on legislation.[44]

Conclusion:

Party membership (including the party's close supporters) may lead people to violate the values of democracy. This causes an extremely limited view of the political spectrum of the country and indicates a loss of a party's ability to judge both what is good from their own party as well as what good may be articulated from the opposite perspective.

Strict party discipline for the last 30 years has transformed the political life into a battlefield of right-minded supporters and hideous enemies. Remember: Democracy requires its citizens be, first, proud Americans! To support a party, one must serve the whole country. Ideas applicable to the whole political spectrum must be the foundation of political solutions. Most of these are arrived at through the process of compromise.

44 Stacey Selleck, "Congress Spends More Time Dialing for Dollars Than on Legislative Work", *US Term Limits*, April 2016

Democratic Principles—Commitment and Participation

What is Your Commitment as a U.S. Citizen?

Let us acknowledge the many committed citizens and politicians who stand for the Democracy of this country. We do need leaders who have the courage to speak their values and their truth.

The United States is a big country, both in terms of area and population, and the needs of its citizens vary greatly depending on the area and its local culture. People are deeply connected, though, by and through the structure and substance of their government.

In *Part 5* of this book is a conclusive call for action providing you with commitments and suggestions that will help you support and strengthen our democracy.

Democratic Principles—Equal Opportunities

Decades of Poverty and No Solution

American society has been unable to resolve the problem of mass poverty all the way back to its foundation. The Organization of Economic Cooperation and Development (OECD) puts the proportion of poor people in the U.S. at 17.8% in 2017.[45] One in five Americans is unable to make a living without support from the government or non-profit organizations. In comparison to other OECD countries, this proportion of the population is much higher and in addition reflects the fact that the United States has the highest number of individuals in poverty. There must be specific reasons why poverty affects such a large proportion of the population, and why it has remained at such persistently high levels for decades.

When Michael Harrington published "The Other America", in 1962, his book evoked astonishment and dismay at the fact that hidden poverty was so widespread in the United States. These facts prompted President Johnson (1963-1968) to launch his "War on Poverty" mentioned in a biography of Harrington.[46] Medicare (health insurance for older or disabled citizens), Medicaid (a healthcare program for low-income citizens), and food stamps for socially disadvantaged persons were the basis for a socially conscious United States; their success remains undisputed.

The problem of poverty has deep roots in American society. Let us look at one aspect of the history of poverty.

The first settlers were mainly Puritans. They belonged to the Protestant movement in Europe and settled in Massachusetts Bay because the British King Henry VIII and his daughter Queen Elizabeth I restricted their religious activities in England. Their faith and conviction were shaped by the doctrine of predestination by Jean Calvin, the French reforming theologist. Predestination is part of the Calvin Christian theology doctrine, which states that all events in life are the will of God. Thus, the Puritans had the

---

45 https://www.statista.com/statistics/233910/poverty-rates-in-oecd-countries/

46 Maurice Issermann, *The other American: The Life of Michael Harrington,* Public Affairs, New York, 2001

deep desire to be the ones chosen by God. This was their commitment to their religion.

This conviction raised by the early settlers created the idea that success in life was a sign of God's will. People believed that success in life was a gift of God or that they were chosen by God to be successful. Success was the proof that they were the chosen ones.

Religion then became the driving force for becoming successful in life, and to secure a spot in heaven. This was the beginning of the dynamic of economic activities. This is the root of the American advantage in inventing, developing, and producing new industrial equipment and thus dominating the economic development in the world.[47]

Now, what about those people who are less successful, or are struggling in life? What is their destiny? Not everybody has that capacity mentally, intellectually, or physically to thrive. Are they being judged as not being chosen by God?

Is it possible that still today, we are judging the less successful or less fortunate and thus have little or no compassion for their situation?

With this mindset, the less successful are left to struggle and their situation is dismissed, or they are constrained to being satisfied with a minimum salary. There is a distinct belief that every human being is responsible for his own destiny. Government assistance is despised and should not be offered.

Presidents Franklin Roosevelt or Lyndon Johnson were the leaders and changemakers of social responsibility and wellbeing of every American citizen. They are the founders of Social

47 Hans-Dieter Gelfert, „Ein doppeltes Erbe hat Amerika gross gemacht. Nun verliert es sich." [A double legacy has made America great. Now it is losing it]. *Neue Zürcher Zeitung,* August 7, 2020

Security, Medicare, and Medicaid. Today, we have more than 200 social programs to help the needy and those who struggle in life.

> The welfare of citizens and their protection is the responsibility of a democratic government. In other words, the legislators are responsible for orchestrating economic and political development that will secure safety and wellbeing, and a basic lifestyle for all American citizens, including the needy. The primary reason we elect political officials is to manage the country and serve its citizens.

I have identified major reasons for the persistence of poverty, and I say poverty has been created and kept in place by institutional mechanisms and sustained, possibly even unconsciously. I call them "poverty traps".[48]

In my view poverty traps are low-paid part-time employment and gig-economy jobs which have no social benefits and no health insurance. Millions of Americans have no pension plans. Finally, the Federal minimum wage creates a vicious cycle of dependency on the 200 plus social programs provided by the Federal government to supplement the insufficient low minimum wage.

---

48 See my book: *Restore Trust, Economic Solutions to Current Social and Political Issues in the U.S.*, 2018

Does the Free Market Economy Still Apply?

The Federal minimum wage has remained frozen at $7.25 since July 2009. This hourly minimum wage is a standard for corporate America and has only recently been challenged. While many states and cities have raised this rate significantly on their own initiative, $15 an hour is not a luxury to afford a decent life working a 40-hour week. Food, housing, clothing, transportation, and healthcare are basic needs. The low minimum wage fixed by Congress, $7.25 an hour, undermines self-esteem and creates a vicious and endless poverty trap. [49]

The Federal authorities specify an income poverty line (the "Federal poverty line"). If workers fall below the line, they are entitled to benefits in the form of food stamps and participation in the Federal programs for free medical treatment by doctors or in hospitals (Medicaid); support programs for school breakfasts (the School Breakfast Program) and lunches (the National School Lunch Program); housing programs (Section 8 Housing Program); Earned Income Tax Credit benefits; and more.[50] All of these programs are funded by taxpayers. The reason employees agree to work for such meager wages is they know they can rely on these government programs. These are personal government subsidies, initiated by the low minimum income wage. Ultimately, you reader, are funding these subsidies.

This phenomenon of subsidized remuneration is widespread across the country. When a large company decides to pay only the

---

49 Neff, *ante*

50 Tim Worstall, "Fantastical Nonsense About WalMart, The Waltons And $7.8 Billion In Tax Breaks", *Forbes*, April 14, 2014

minimum wage set by the state in a certain region, local businesses follow suit.

In short, state's Social Service Departments become responsible to fill the gap between the minimum salary and a most basic living income. Let me explain: an employer who pays minimum salaries immediately initiates the enrollment by its employees in government programs. It is not exaggeration to say that private companies determine how taxpayer's money is spent.

> A free market economy is totally self-sustaining and does not rely on government subsidies in any form. In the above examples, the taxpayer is paying for the gap filled by government programs.

Wage subsidies provided by the government do not belong in a free market economy. A minimum wage that is set too low triggers the need for government assistance and may create poverty, which in turn leads to increased spending on social benefits. Consequently, the proper way to fight poverty is by simply paying fair market-rate wages.

As it is in place currently, the wage structure with minimum wage and government subsidies are typical of a socialist economy. It is the opposite of the market principles so often taught by American economists. If the self-regulation of the free market mechanism really worked, there would be no need to set minimum wages at all. I call this an economic thinking error.

Why is this point simply overlooked?

Additionally, the controversy of welfare payments made to large corporations for employing minimum wage recipients does not represent a free market economy. Showbiz *CheatSheet* cites the numbers for Boeing ($13.8 billion) and lists other companies, such as Alcoa, Intel, General Motors, Ford, Fiat Chrysler Corporation, Royal Dutch Shell, and Nike.[51]

The Dwindling Middle Class

Since the 1980s, poor and middle-class income groups have stagnated, and their incomes, when adjusted to account for relative purchasing power, remains the same or even declines. In the same period, the income of the rich and the richest income groups have increased significantly. This amounts to a polarization between rich and poor, and to the hollowing-out of the middle class. This phenomenon can be seen in many regions around the world, but it is most pronounced in this country.

The stagnation of middle-class income is explained by the assertion that the productivity gains achieved in the manufacturing and service sectors are solely attributable to capital owners. The rich, and the extremely rich, manage to increase their shares of the value produced in the economic process, while the other partners in this process—namely the workers and employees—and, above all, unskilled workers—are left empty-handed.[52]

51 Sam Becker, The 8 Biggest Corporate Welfare Recipients in America, *ShowBiz CheatSheet*, June 20, 2017

52 Amand Giridharadas, *Winners Take All, The Elite Charade of Changing the World*, (New York: Vintage Books, 2019)

Part 4: Current Political Issues

American Legislation and Democracy in Action

American law was originally based on English common law. After the Constitution of the United States came into effect, the common law—along with various Federal laws and international treaties—formed the basis of American law. The Constitution is considered the highest legal authority in the country, and every single law must comply with the Constitution and its principles. It is ultimately the Supreme Court's job to safeguard this compliance. If new developments occur, the Supreme Court is responsible to reassess the laws of previous rulings and determine how the laws will be interpreted going forward. The interpretation of each individual Justice toward these new developments plays a key role in the outcome of their decisions.

All details and all possible exceptions are attempted to be stated in the laws. Senators or Representatives will often only vote for a bill that comes before them if their requests for exceptions are being considered. As a result, the laws are comprehensive and, at the same time, may contain substance that is controversial for other legislators.

It is generally impossible for the ordinary citizen to get the slightest understanding of what is written unless he or she is an attorney. The many pages of our statutes filled with complex provisions are used by specialists and lobbyists to interpret the law in favor of their own desired outcomes.

For example, the Patient Protection and Affordable Care Act, the law introducing compulsory health insurance known as Obamacare, was 906 pages long. The document *For The People Act of 2019*, sponsored by Representative John Sarbanes (D, Maryland), introduced on January 3, 2019, was approximately 700 pages in length.

2020, the Year of Democratic Uprising

The case of George Floyd, whose forceful arrest in May 2020, has shocked the country and the world. Floyd, a Black citizen, was arrested on May 25, 2020 allegedly because he used a counterfeit $20 bill. Four police officers in Minneapolis arrested him, and one of the officers kneeled down to press his knee on Floyd's neck for several minutes, while Floyd begged for his life several times, saying, "I can't breathe".

These words have become the slogan for national and international protests around police brutality, racism, and prejudice. The case of George Floyd is bringing to light the present racism and covert inequality toward people of color. The current reality is that racism is no longer tolerated by a majority of American people and, specifically, by the younger generations who, since June 2020, have been filling the streets protesting.

This country fought a brutal Civil War 155 years ago, which ended when Southern General Robert E. Lee surrendered his Confederate Army to General Ulysses S. Grant as commander of the Union troops. This occurred on April 9, 1865, in the State of Virginia.

As a consequence of the end of the war, all slaves were freed, the last one on June 19, 1865 in Texas. The holiday which acknowledges that event—Juneteenth—was first celebrated by freed slaves in Texas in 1866; this year will mark the 155th anniversary of the original date.

Today, 155 years later, we still have human beings in this country who do not treat all Americans with the same respect, the same honor, the same dignity, and the same kindness. In this day and age, we cannot tolerate suppression, poverty, or inequality.

High Level Crime—Obstruction of Justice

George Floyd's death was far from an isolated incident in this country. On February 23, 2020, Ahmaud Arbery, a young Black man jogging in his hometown in Georgia, was shot in the street by two White men, Gregory and Travis McMichael, while they were driving their truck. They said they believed they were pursuing an intruder in their neighborhood. The two pursuers were father and son, a retired police officer and a sporting goods store owner. When a dispute arose between the jogger, who was unarmed, and the pursuers, they killed him on the spot.

Local police authorities were advised in late February by the District Attorney to make no arrest, which was again the advice on April 2, 2020, after the case was reviewed a second time. The fact that the father, Gregory McMichael, was a former clerk to the District Attorney changed the assessment, and the case was transferred to a neighboring District Attorney's Office. It took six weeks for authorities to realize they had a conflict of interest and would eventually have to deal with a murder case.

Meanwhile, a video from a third-party driver who filmed the scene with the three men was handed to an attorney. The video went public and viral two months after the shooting. The video shows the jogger passing a white truck where two men talked to him and then shot him. There were no signs of any aggressive movements by Arbery.

Finally, in early May, the Georgia governor agreed to involve the Georgia Bureau of Investigation in this case. This authority decided, on May 7, to arrest the two shooters with a charge of felony murder and aggravated assault. Interestingly, they arrested the filming driver at the end of May and charged him with the same charges.

At this writing, it is expected that a trial will be held that classifies the shooting as murder, and a just sentence will be imposed.

What is surprising and shocking is the handling of the case by the local police and the Judicial District's Office. For two months, the shooters—if not to say "murderers"—went about their daily lives without any restrictions.

Apparently, the values of fairness and honesty have been replaced by bias and incompetence. If legally qualified officials can commit such violations of the law, there is no question that favoritism, inequality, and racism played a role. Did the authority truly think that an investigation into this case was not necessary? Were they trying to get away with this glaring ignorance of the law? If a Black man is murdered, do the rules for justice and democracy no longer apply?

The systematic injustice against Black people has cost far too many lives: Rayshard Brooks, Breonna Taylor, Alton Sterling, Eric Garner, Freddy Gray and many more. The legal consequences often end in acquittals that violate the letter and spirit of democracy.

Democratic Values—All People Deserve Equal Treatment

The next observation of injustice highlights the vicious cycles created by lawmakers and the judicial system, ranging from sentencing to incarcerations. Generally, in many parts of the country, people of color are badly treated in the courts, as their sentences are longer compared to Whites committing the same crimes. Black men's incarceration rate is six times the rate of Whites in the U.S.[53] Even though the total number of imprisoned people has been in decline by 15% over the last decade, ours is still the highest number worldwide, with 431 prisoners per 100,000 individuals. The total U.S. population is 327 million, of which 1.4 million people are incarcerated.[54] This is five times the number of incarcerations in 1980. Moreover, much of our income from taxes goes to policing and incarcerations: a law in 1994 funded 100,000 more policemen and $10 billion for new penitentiary buildings alone.

Once in prison, people of color are caught in the vicious cycle of quick indictment, longer prison terms, and social isolation. When they are released from prison, re-integration into family and society is the first obstacle. Unemployment, mental illness, poverty, and finally, a high relapse rate, is very common.[55] So common, in fact, that a well-known law—the "Three strikes"

---

53 E. Ann Carson, Prisoners in 2018, U.S. Department of Justice, Office of Justice Programs, Bureau of Justice Statistics, April 2020, https://www.bjs.gov/content/pub/pdf/p18.pdf

54 *Ibid.*

55 Meret Baumann, Warum Schwarze in den USA für das gleiche Delikt öfter verurteilt werden und länger im Gefängnis sitzen als Weisse (Why Black People in the U.S. are more often Convicted of the Same Offense and Spend Longer Time in Prison than White People), *Neue Zürcher Zeitung*, June 20, 2020

rule—passed by President Clinton, who wanted to be known as "tough on crime", brought lifelong prison sentences for relapsed perpetrators.

President Nixon's Law and Order policy assured his election in 1968. He declared a "War on Drugs" in 1971, which resulted in a huge increase of indictments for marijuana and heroin possessions. In 1986, President Reagan signed the Anti-Drug Abuse Act, known as the 100-to-1-rule, which sentenced the possession of crack to 100 days, compared to one day in prison for possession of powder cocaine. Crack was highly addictive and of low cost, and was mainly consumed by Black people, while the more expensive powder cocaine was typically consumed by White, high-income people.

As a result, the Black communities were heavily impacted by this radical shift in drug control, and it was considered racially biased as a wave of arrests and overly long convictions followed the signing of the law. In 1995, the Sentencing Commission checked into the problem of the bias charges for similar cases. It took them until October 2010 to correct the unfair sentencing between crack and cocaine, when President Obama signed the Fair Sentencing Act. Now the ratio between the two drug violations was fixed at 18-to-1, and the minimum sentencing was reduced.

In 2017, a study showed that, if we applied the same strict sentencing guidelines for Black and other people of color, and White people, we would reduce the overall number of imprisoned people by 9% in Federal penitentiary facilities.[56]

---

[56] Christopher Ingraham, Black men sentenced to more time for committing the exact same crime as a White person, study finds, *The Washington Post*, November 16, 2017, https://www.washintonpost.com/news/wonk/wp/2017/11/16/black-men-sentenced-to-more-time-for-committing-the-exact-same-crime-as-a-white-person-study-finds/

"All men are created equal" says the Declaration of Independence of 1776, and the right to justice and a fair trial in accord with the Magna Carta Libertate of 1215 are part of our Constitution. These noble principles are not being fulfilled.

Hidden Injustice—Voter Suppression

Alexander the Great was advised by the oracle of the Egyptian god, Amon-Ra, to "rule with justice and respect for those under his power".[57] Why shouldn't this apply to American political lawmakers and jurists? Humanity must always be guided by the highest ideals—certainly in the first country to have deliberately articulated those principles in the documents of origin—as this is the only way such a carefully guided nation can achieve the great deeds its Founders fought to bring to life.

Voting restrictions are mainly affected toward minorities, Black people, Native Americans, and low-income people who are already struggling to have their voices heard. Voting restrictions are intentional, and the motive to restrict the right of others cannot be pure. Is it the party that is leading this injustice, or is it racially or economically motivated? I would say it takes a significant number of people, from politicians to civil servants and volunteers, who deliberately or unconsciously execute such orders.

Civil servants working at the 50 state departments, and people with legal training, mastering the subject of legislation and in charge of designing voting rights—intentionally manipulate those rights to their advantage. As mentioned before, nearly 400 voting restrictions laws have been passed between the years

57 J. Rufus Fears, *"The Wisdom of History"*, Lecture 12 on Alexander the Great and the Middle East (Chantilly, VA: *The Teaching Company*, 2007), p. 60

2011 and 2015 or eight per state.[58] Are these civil servants or employees resigned or complicit in undercutting democratic principles?

Given the lack of consideration by so-called leaders who themselves corrupt the very spirit of democracy and are charged with training poll workers, it is not surprising that the ideas of racism and injustice are more developed than the need for democracy and justice. We count on our political leaders to be unbiased and impartial to voting results. Politicians who are not committed to a democratic voting process are, in fact, betraying American citizens. We cannot any longer tolerate this hidden kind of injustice, as it is a breeding ground for racism and inequalities.

It is anti-democratic thinking at many levels of the American political establishment that distorts and restricts the elections in the states to such an extent that the idea of an intentional obstruction of the election process becomes apparent. It appears that democratic values have been overcome by racist prejudice. The big problem is anti-democratic thinking and acting, which explains not only the alarming incidents affecting the elections, but also the unjust treatment of Black people by police and political and judicial authorities. It is worrying that, in the cradle of modern democracy, democracy is either not implemented or is not respected in practice.

Injustices and unfair advantages are introduced into American laws in such a way that they may no longer be recognized as such. Compliance with twisted rules gives these statutes an air of legality.

The Founding Fathers referred to the Athenian and Roman examples to form the young country in 1776. Many of their

---

58 Ari Berman, *ante*

original intentions have not been passed on through time. Civics, a social science dealing with the rights and obligations of citizenship, is of low importance at any level of education. What is lacking is a fundamental conviction in democratic coexistence. Small, undemocratic habits and behaviors have become routine and crept in everywhere—and we got used to it!

Alexander the Great disagreed with the view of his teacher and mentor, Aristotle, who believed the Greeks were superior to other peoples, whom he called barbarians. Alexander saw every character as a valuable person: "He believed that people should be judged on the basis of their character, not their race or ethnicity".[59] This idea was adapted to the Declaration of Independence and we have to see today that elected officials and American jurists are not living by these ideals.

Conclusion

The ideas and values of true democracy are poorly established within American society. The idea of democracy is much more than the limited outcome of elections, where only if the victory falls to your party is it considered to be democratic.

Winning or losing an election is part of the democratic process. All parties have to search for arguments to convince citizens to vote for them. Democratic processes require constant adjustments for solutions that concern the people who will be voting.

People who are manipulating the voting process on any level are abusing democratic rights, and they are taking the law into their own hands. Party leaders or politicians have hundreds of assistants helping them fulfill their goals to win the election.

59 *Ibid.*

Politicians are more and more "party soldiers" and not leaders who know democratic values.

The fact that conflicts of interest and gerrymandering in favor of one political party are not perceived as wrong shows fundamental gaps in the respect for and practice of democracy. In addition to the political circles, the judicial system and police authorities are filled with undemocratic and, therefore, unhumanitarian principles.

Legislation at various levels of the nation have undemocratic values woven through the legal processes into detailed laws that can no longer be challenged or sued. Whether tax advantages, the use of force, or exemptions from health insurance, individual interests are encapsulated in laws in a legal decision-making process so that they are unassailable.

The Origin of Hate Groups

Part of the concept of freedom in the United States is the right to express your opinion and act according to your own beliefs and principles. Under these conditions, fringe ideas can take on a life of their own and gain power.

One notable example is hate groups. These embrace extreme ideologies and live out their principles and beliefs both publicly and clandestinely. The list of hate groups includes the Ku Klux Klan (who seek to enforce the supremacy of the White race), Black Separatist, Racist Skinhead, White Nationalist, Neo-Nazi, Neo-Confederate, Christian Identity, and Anti-LGBT groups, among others.

The geographical distribution shows a concentration of these associations from the east coast to the Wisconsin-Illinois-Missouri-Oklahoma line, and in the south all the way west to Texas. The other half of the Midwest to the west coast is almost free of hate groups, except for California. A total of 892 active hate groups and 998 protest groups against the government are active in this country.[60]

The number of these groups increased sharply during Barack Obama's Presidency. Between 2001 and 2008, an average of around 160 groups were active; this number grew to almost 1,360 in the period between 2009 and 2015. The Southern Poverty Law Center counted 1,020 such groups in 2019.[61]

The Federal Bureau of Investigation (FBI) defines such groups as: "A hate group is a social group that advocates and practices hatred, hostility, or violence towards members of a race, ethnicity, nation, religion, gender, gender identity, sexual orientation or any other designated sector of society." According to the FBI, a hate group's primary purpose is "to promote animosity, hostility, and malice against persons belonging to a race, religion, disability, sexual orientation, or ethnicity/national origin which differs from that of the members of the organization."[62]

For an assessment from the perspective of an ideal democracy, it is interesting to know what these groups are aiming for. They are classified as far-right or conservative, or with the designation "alt-right". Their behavior is described as "a weird mix of old-school neo-Nazi, conspiracy theorists, anti-globalists, and

60 Southern Poverty Law Center (SPLC), 2015

61 Southern Poverty Law Center (SPLC), 2019, https://www.splcenter.org/hate-map

62 "Hate Crime Data Collection Guidelines", Uniform Crime Reporting: Summary Reporting System: National Incident-Based Reporting System, U.S. Department of Justice: Federal Bureau of Investigation, Criminal Justice Information Services Division, revised October 1999

young right-wing internet trolls—all united in the belief that White male identity is under attack by 'multicultural, politically correct' forces".[63] Thus, according to the FBI, their aim, broadly stated, would be the preservation of White male identity.

They exert their influence both through intellectual manipulation and violence. There are innumerable classifications of hate groups, yet what is most important in terms of their motivation for action is the division into those who propagate hate speech and those who commit hate crimes. When physical violence is used, the FBI gets involved.

In terms of group dynamics, the starting point is always hate speech. This is how verbal violence is defined: "the use of extreme language against an individual or a group that either implies a direct threat that physical force will be used against them or is seen as an indirect call for others to use it".[64]

In their ideological world, group members have a sense of belonging to the group and differentiate themselves from outsiders. Group identity is important. One survey claims that receiving respect and validation within a group is more important to members than the actual hatred toward other groups.[65] Could it be that these members are lonely people and just looking to belong somewhere?

Religious hate groups are odd. It is striking that there are Christian and Muslim groups who turn the "Love Thy Neighbor" principle—as taught by their respective religions—into hate.

---

63 *The Week Staff*, "The Rise of the alt-right", *The Week*. Retrieved 17 December 2016. https://theweek.com/articles/651929/rise-altright

64 Sprinzak, Ehud, *Brother against Brother: Violence and Extremism in Israeli Politics from Altalena to the Rabin Assassination* (New York: *The Free Press*, 1999)

65 Parker, M.T. and Janoff-Bulman, R. , "Lessons from morality-based social identity: the power of outgroup 'hate,' not just ingroup 'love'", *Social Justice Research* 26: 81–96, 2013, doi:10.1007/s11211-012-0175-6

Where Does the Hate Originate? First Settlements? Civil War?

In the case of American hate groups, their fears may very well hark back to the conquest of the country—as immigrants entered unfamiliar areas, they encountered indigenous peoples, Indians, who were not willing to give up their land without a fight. It was a life and death struggle on both sides. The survival mode of the first settlers dominates the American character up to today.

Especially (but not only) in the South of the young United States, this racist conviction was directed at Black people, who had been brought against their own will to America, as slaves. "Throughout the history of the United States, race has been used by Whites for legitimizing and creating difference and social, economic, and political, exclusion".[66] Clear statements about the alleged White super-human can be found in legal texts: U.S. immigration laws prior to 1965 clearly declared that, "Northern Europeans are a superior subspecies of the white race".[67]

The Cruel Reality of Slavery and Life in the South

From the late 16th to early 19th century, slavery was part of a triangle trade between Europe, West Africa, and the Americas. Ships traded European commodities to West-Africa, loaded slaves for Brazil, the Caribbean, and the United States, and finally trans-

66 Leland T. Saito, *Race and Politics: Asian Americans, Latinos, and Whites in a Los Angeles Suburb* (Champaign: University of Illinois Press, 1998), p. 154

67 Jennifer Ludden, "1965 immigration law changed face of America", *NPR, 2006*

ported sugar, whiskey, cotton, and tobacco to Europe. The slaves were abducted in Africa or sold by local African leaders to European traders and shipped in chains by boat to the Americas.[68]

The first slaves, human beings, arrived from Spain in 1502, at Hispaniola (today Greater Antilles). In 1619, they were sold in Virginia to plantation owners as cheap labor. They were traded as "commodities", and regardless of age or family connections. Food and shelter were supplied, but no pay for the hard work in the cotton, sugar, and tobacco fields. No pay either for the talented men and women, those with special skills, such as carpentry, cooking, or sewing, which added value and huge benefits to their owners. The hard work performed by the slaves was considered added wealth to the plantation owners.

While the Declaration of Independence of 1776 postulated that all people were created equal, there was no mention of slavery or Black people in the document whatsoever. The treatment of Blacks, the holding of slaves by White people and leaders, today we consider one of the strongest weaknesses and wrongdoings of those days.

It was only when the Constitutional Convention of 1787, in Philadelphia, discussed that the number of representatives for each state in the House of Representatives would be determined by the total numbers of residents, that the Blacks were even acknowledged: to increase the number of representatives in the House, it was beneficial to include the slaves as residents. Still there was a huge gap, as for the White people the count was one to one, and only 60% of the slaves were counted as residents, with the intention to get the necessary seats. The slaves had no

68 Zora Neale Hurston, *Barracoon, The Story of the Last "Black Cargo"* (New York: Amistad Press, 2018), and Joel K. Bourne, Jr., et al., *Last Journey into Slavery,* National Geographic, February 2020

voting rights. The sole interest of the individual state was to have as many representatives as possible.

Finally, by 1805, some of the northern states managed to eliminate slavery. However, vicious racism existed all over the country; even in the northern states there were accounts of abuse of those who had escaped or were free of bondage. The South, with its plantation-based economy, was unwilling to let go of slavery as it supported their rich lifestyle and their accumulation of wealth.

The conflict between the industrialized North and the agrarian South was caused mainly by the slave issue and the difference in principles and values. The conflict ultimately led to secession by the southern states, the formation of the Confederate States of America and, thereafter, to the Civil War.

While the northern states were far superior in terms of materiel and personnel, the southern states had the better trained officers and, since they were in defense of their territory and their right to own slaves, they were motivated to fight and win at all cost. The South was defending a society of which slavery was an integral part, and in their eyes, it was their right.

The war was long, until the North—led by President Abraham Lincoln—prevailed in 1865 and saved the Union. When President Lincoln signed the Emancipation Proclamation on September 22, 1862, he changed the status under Federal Law for more than three million Black slaves in the secessionist South.

The Proclamation was also a military measure. Black soldiers were integrated into the Union Army. This was a major ideological shift for the Union Army, as it fought now to end slavery. The South lost the war, and, with that, the Confederate States of America collapsed, which resulted in the abolition of slavery.[69]

---

69 As depicted in Steven Spielberg, "Lincoln", movie, 2012

In December 1865, Congress approved the Thirteenth Amendment abolishing slavery and involuntary servitude. President Lincoln paid for his courage with his life, as he was assassinated mere days after the end of the war.

At the end of the war, the Confederate South was largely devastated and destroyed (*e.g.,* by General Sherman's March to the Sea), and its White population were humiliated. The treatment of White southern political leaders after the Civil war was lenient; none of them was tried for treason.

Many former slaves, now legally freed, were, in broad political terms, energized and jubilant at war's end. During Reconstruction, which lasted 11 years, from 1865 through 1876, the freed former slaves achieved significant political power across the former confederacy. Sixteen Black men were elected to the U.S. Congress from the southern states during Reconstruction. White supremacists in the south were unwilling to let go of their beliefs—they continued to believe in white supremacy and were openly allowed to propagate their views.

Union troops and government officials were in the South for those 11 years, enforcing the values, methods, and government practices of the North. With the Compromise of 1877, Rutherford B. Hayes gained the electoral votes of the Southern states to become President (1877—1881) by promising to withdraw the Union soldiers from the South. That deal included the end of Reconstruction, and the end of the Union intervention, which changed the fate of Black people for the next 88 years. The long war, the fight for the freedom of the slaves, the many lives lost, seemed all for nothing.

How did the leaders of those days, our forefathers, tolerate such a betrayal on the people?

White supremacists terrorized Blacks into political submission. The southern states thwarted the pursued equality of the former slaves as much as they could, by introducing laws (Black Codes, later Jim Crow laws) that made it impossible for the freed slaves to have a say in politics or to improve their social and economic standing. Southern White people resorted to intimidation and even murder, *e.g.,* through the Ku Klux Klan, which was founded in 1866 and quickly became the organization for southern White underground resistance. A state of racial terror continued until the modern civil rights movement challenged it—about 70 years later.

In my opinion, the consequences of the Civil War, the losses of the war, the loss of power, and the abolition of slavery, as well as the dissolution of the Confederate States of America, are the underlying causes of resentment and anger today. It seems that there was never a real reconciliation between the winners and losers of the Civil War. Resentment, bitterness, and hostility has been the result. White southerners were stripped of their beliefs and of the right to own slaves, which resulted in their losing their superiority over Black people. Some White southerners have not overcome that loss, that defeat of power and, thus, they exert hate and resentment to this day.

The real equality of all races under the law had to wait 100 more years, until 1964, when President Johnson (1963-1968) pushed the civil rights laws through Congress. It was the civil rights movement that fought against the prohibition of mixed marriage and racial segregation in public transportation, as well as public locations. The movement opposed the denial of political and social freedom for the Blacks.

In some parts of the United States, the population who were considered non-White were deprived of the right to vote, barred from government office, and prevented from holding most government jobs well into the second half of the 20th century. In practice, the goal of equality has not yet been achieved in many parts of the country.

The election of Barack Obama as President in 2008 triggered feelings of fear, hate, and anger in certain American cultures. The election of a Black man as President sparked the increase of hate groups exponentially, with a concentration in the former Confederate states, compared to the Presidency of G.W. Bush (2000-2008).[70]

In July 2017, the Confederate flag was raised in South Carolina. In August 2017, a demonstration against the demolition of a statue of Confederate General Robert E. Lee escalated in Charlottesville, Virginia, which resulted in one person dying and many injured. Recent protests around the conflict of the Confederate flags and the destruction of statues revealed deep, old hurt and anger toward White supremacy. Today, young people of all colors and background take to the streets to fight for equality. They are unwilling to tolerate racial inequality.

The demographic change caused by immigration, primarily from Latin America and Asia, and higher birth rates among immigrants, has led to a decrease in the proportion of the White population. If the trend continues, the proportion of Whites will fall below the 50% threshold in twenty or thirty years.

Hate in a Democracy

Tolerating hate groups is inconsistent with the ideals of democracy and, in fact, it is pure poison for any society. Some of these hate groups appear to be protecting the freedom of the American

70 Southern Poverty Law Center, https://www.splcenter.org/hate-map

people and the Constitution, and in the process are totally disrespecting democratic principles.

This is an old pattern of getting what you want with force, and it is a sign of a low level of consciousness. We must appease people with such deep hate and provide them with skills and tools to make their lives easier. We must support people in raising their standards of living and provide them with education.

The best tools for this job are information, education, and the alleviation of poverty. The Southern Poverty Law Center promotes its efforts with the slogan: Fighting Hate—Teaching Tolerance—Seeking Justice.[71] Another group is Teaching Tolerance, which has a particular focus on working with school-aged children across the country.[72] Both try to raise awareness of the problems of hate through education in schools and communities. The group reaches out to teachers, students, and social workers, to make them well-aware of the issues surrounding hate, and the group trains students and others with courses, podcasts, webinars, and self-study tools.

Admittedly, the number of hate group members is small compared to the overall population, but their influence is greater than their numbers might suggest. More importantly, the effects and consequences that these expressions of hate have on the society are destructive and often fatal for some.

This country is being permeated by the spirit of hate toward fellow citizens of different skin colors, religious beliefs, and political preferences. Supporters of the two major political parties are hostile toward each other publicly and on social media. Where

---

71 https://www.charities.org/news/blog/southern-poverty-law-center-fighting-hate-teaching-tolerance-seeking-justice

72 https://www.tolerance.org/the-moment/december-11-2018-fighting-hate-at-schools

does this leave the average American, who is looking for a peaceful life?

Why do some citizens turn toward an ideal based on race, religion, or ideology and not toward the ideal of being a citizen of the United States, or at least a Texan, a Californian, or a citizen of Oregon, or of any other state?

Conclusion:

The weaknesses of human beings are judgment, blame, shame, evaluation, and discrimination. It takes leadership to raise the consciousness on all levels.

Urgent and Important

This country has unique challenges. Whether it is mass shootings, drug abuse, a real estate crisis, a stock market crash, a lack of health insurance, or poverty, some of these circumstances have been created or neglected by government regulations. Everything you do, and do not do, has an impact on everything else.

Gun Ownership and Mass Shootings

The number of guns in the hands of civilians is extremely high. Gun ownership is legal, with licensing for hunters and recreational shooters. Another group feels the need to own guns for self-protection. However, there is a third group of gun owners who use their guns as instruments of aggression. The Second

Amendment establishes the right to own firearms as part of the Bill of Rights from 1791.

> "A well-regulated Militia, being necessary to the security of a free State, the right of the people to keep and bear Arms, shall not be infringed."

Whether this right has contributed to the mass shootings that have taken place in too many schools (Virginia Tech 2007, Sandy Hook, CT 2012, Parkland FL, Houston TX), in churches, and in Las Vegas, it has been the subject of long-standing debates. The widespread possession of any kind of arms is today a real problem.

In times of increasing uncertainty, the rush toward gun ownership is likely to become even more pronounced. Indeed, reports from California, for example, show just that: During the state of emergency and the lock-down due to COVID-19 in Pacifica, near San Francisco, many people—most of them young males—swarmed to gun stores. "I don't trust the government to get the Corona crisis under control.... Chaos will break out and there will be panic, just like there was in the supermarkets. I have to be able to defend myself if that happens".[73] Newspaper articles in the *San Francisco Chronicle* confirm the run on gun stores. Apparently, gun ownership gives many people a sense of security in uncertain times.

73 Marie-Astrid Langer, "In Kalifornien stürmen die Bürger die Waffenläden" [In California, citizens swarm the gun stores], *Neue Zürcher Zeitung*, March 20, 2020

Drugs

The Food and Drug Administration (FDA) "is responsible for protecting the public health by ensuring the safety, efficacy, and security of human and veterinary drugs, biological products, and medical devices; and by ensuring the safety of our nation's food supply, cosmetics, and products that emit radiation."[74]

However, the FDA has only partially fulfilled its responsibility for the public health. For example, Purdue Pharma L.P. and other companies sold painkillers in irrational and irresponsible quantities even though they had been classified as dangerous as early as 1960. Consumption was extremely high. Doctors and pharmacies were lured in with bonuses to boost sales. One district in Oklahoma reported sales volumes totaling more than 1,000 tablets per capita each year—that means 1,000 pills for every single American every year. The FDA failed to notice that this widespread use of the analgesic medication had nothing to do with health, but addiction.

Primarily, Democratic politicians from Connecticut were supported by Purdue Pharma L.P. When inquiries by the FDA were made into Perdue's OxyContin, the company's blockbuster, the need for further investigation was suppressed.[75] The unrestricted availability over decades led to widespread consumption throughout the country. Finally, in summer 2019, 48 states and Washington, D.C. sued the company, which then filed for

74 https://www.fda.gov/about-fda/what-we-do

75 Daniela Altimari, The Sackler family, who own OxyContin (maker Perdue Pharma), donated generously to Connecticut Democrats, Hartford Courant, January 18, 2019, https://www.courant.com/politics/hc-pol-purdue-pharma-democratic-donations-20190118-fcvxe-quuozdgvkrnek4tbex5jq-story.html

bankruptcy to implement settlements and final resolutions of litigations. The death toll since 1995 is estimated at 750,000.[76]

The Subprime Mortgage Crisis of 2006 to 2008

The American subprime mortgage crisis of 2006 to 2008 was devastating for many homeowners. About 10 million Americans lost their jobs, and 3.8 million homeowners found their homes foreclosed, which, at that time was every 54th home.[77]

Requests for real estate loans were handled irresponsibly, but also negligently and against the logical principles of credit checking. If you wanted to finance a house, you were asked if you also wanted to, perhaps, buy a new car. Some consultants even recommended including the costs of weddings in the loan amount.

A legitimate credit check usually consists of two components: first, the bank has to ensure that the value of the house is significantly higher than the mortgage, and second, it has to be assured the burden of interest and principal payments is appropriate for the borrower. For this purpose, the relevant construction documents (plans, cost estimates, sales prices) must be submitted and the house must be inspected. The new mortgage customer must be able to demonstrate solvency in the long term; to do this, they must have their incomes and assets checked.

---

76 The Drug Overdose Epidemic: Behind the Numbers. Centers for Disease Control and Prevention, at https://www.cdc.gov/drugoverdose/data/index.html

77 Colleen Shelby, The financial crises hit 10 years ago. For some, it feels like yesterday, *The Los Angeles Times*, September 15, 2018

Between 2004 and 2008, however, hardly any serious checks were carried out. There was an inflated mortgage volume. As banks and insurance companies, as well as hedge funds were involved in the speculation, the financial situation became complex.

The real estate market assumes that real estate prices will keep on rising indefinitely. Anyone who buys today will be able to sell at a higher price in the near or distant future.

These assumptions came to an abrupt halt when no buyers were willing to buy real estate at sharply rising prices. In September 2008, the collapse of the mortgage market triggered a chain reaction, which led to the collapse of investment banks, including the giant Lehman Brothers. This crisis also swept away several insurance companies. There was fear that this American crisis would affect and collapse the entire economic system worldwide.

Lack of Health Insurance Coverage

About 10% of the population, or 30 million Americans, have no health insurance coverage whatsoever. In addition, about 30% are insured by their employers, but if and when they are terminated, their insurance coverage would end. The impact is clearly visible now in 2020, with the Covid19 epidemic resulting in millions of people losing their employment.

President Obama (2008-2016) was able to introduce mandatory health insurance in 2010, known as Obamacare. The intention was to offer a basic health care coverage to all Americans. This severely undermined Obama's approval ratings among voters.

The majority of the population did not understand that this was a system based on solidarity. Here is how it works: if 100% of the population buys health insurance, the cost for each participant will be much lower. It is understandable that young people most likely are healthy and will not benefit from the services right now as much as the older generations. Healthy people refused to participate in that system. Obama's presidency suffered under these conditions.

The benefits of the intended general health insurance, with the inclusion of pre-existing conditions, are widely recognized and appreciated by families today. Unfortunately, mandatory health insurance has been abolished and a variety of Federal support payments have been significantly reduced since 2017.

The Privilege to Pay no Taxes

Paying little or no tax is a major goal for many, worldwide. Historically, the granting of tax privileges was not limited to the aristocratic social order that ended with the French Revolution in 1789.

The key question of every form of government is how to make it so that most individuals in the hierarchical levels remain loyal to the government system, or the ruler, in their daily lives. In order to achieve and maintain this ideal condition with many loyal subordinates, these representatives are provided with rewards and benefits. This is where tax privileges come in.

Every tax break creates privileges, which connote a sense of nobility or aristocracy. The republican tradition of the United States—as opposed to a kingdom—clearly and consciously sought to eliminate the aristocratic element of government.

Are we seeing a revival of aristocratic conditions which were hidden or suppressed in the past? The U.S. Congress has approved laws that grant privileges with aristocratic features to certain groups. Are the American people willing to break with the republican principles that have served the country so well for over 200 years?

The desire for power, absolute rule, and the selfishness of politicians has become increasingly prevalent over the last several decades, with remarkable consequences. "We have the agenda!" in a statement by party leaders that exemplifies the final goal of the American party system: to govern alone and to impose your own party's program on all others.

The founders of the United States of America had the goal to abolish the old European order and introduce modern republican and democratic values. Today, the wealthy have taken on habits of the nobles and behave exactly like them. They pay little-to-no taxes and seem to have more rights than other people. The exercise of power is seen as an ego trip, and it is all about defending and expanding their own advantages.

Now What?

Here, above, I have shared with you the impact the absence of democratic thinking, speaking, and acting has on the American people. It is a deep loss. This country has slowly drifted away from its democratic principles, as they were designed by our Founding Fathers. Some states have never fully accepted or shifted to the guidelines of democracy. If you study the ideas of the Declaration of Independence and the Constitution, you can see that we are far from what they intended to create for the United States of America.

This chapter addresses how to reform some fundamentals in our current politics, with the overall intention of returning us to the roots of American Democracy. The extreme dissatisfaction and frustration about the many unsolved issues and challenges with which we are faced today, could drive the country into deeper imbalance.

The United States of America has been an idol all over the world for decades. The success of WWII established the United States as a leader. The country was thriving on new ideas, inventions, and markets, and this internal strength and economic and social development became the ideal of other nations. They were yearning for the American way of life.

Now, reforms must be initiated and executed according to the guidelines of the Constitution and supporting legislation. Reforms and adjustments must be focused on County, State, and Federal governments alike. A program of activities might be something like the Powell Memo,[78] when all kinds of political groups have the same goal—liberals and conservatives, groups and parties, anti-hate groups, tax groups, anti-racist groups, churches, universities, think tanks, etc.—until a clear understanding of workability is agreed on. I invite you to revisit the original democratic spirit of the United States of America, which lives in the souls and hearts of most Americans.

Here is a quote from John Adams, the second President of the United States:

> "The Revolution was effected before the war commenced. The Revolution was in the minds and hearts of the people; a change in their religious sentiments of their duties and obligations. While the King, and all in Authority under him, were believed to govern, in Justice and

78 Confidential memorandum of August 1971 from Lewis Powell to Eugene Sydnor Jr., Director of the U.S. Chamber of Commerce entitled "Attack on the American Free Enterprise System", calling corporate America to become more aggressive in molding society's thinking about business, politics, government, and the law.

> Mercy according to the Laws and Constitutions derived to them from the God of Nature, and transmitted to them by their Ancestors—they thought themselves bound to pray for the King and Queen and all the Royal Family, and all the Authority under them, as Ministers ordained of God for their good. But when they Saw those Powers renouncing all the Principles of Authority, and bent up on the destruction of all the Securities of their Lives, Liberties and Properties, they thought it their Duty to pray for the Continental Congress and all the thirteen State Congresses, &c".[79]

Are we willing and capable of translating this quotation into a broad movement and re-evaluate democracy and democratic principles?

From the lecture *American Ideals: Founding a "Republic of Virtue,"* by Daniel N. Robinson, I like to quote the following phrases:

> "The America at the founding is a communitarian America, colonists who understood their obligations are chiefly to each other....These were communities that understood themselves largely in Christian terms, very much in the patrimony of the Puritan fathers, understanding that a community of people must live together in such a way as to put private interest and self-interest aside, and to operate in behalf of the good of the whole".[80]

Interestingly, Mr. Robinson continues with the statement that the ideas and idols of a democratic society were anticipated

---

79 John Adams, Letter to Mr. Hezekiah Niles, February 13, 1818, at https://founders.archives.gov/documents/Adams/99-02-02-6854, quoted partially by Daniel N. Robinson, *ante*, p. 9

80 Robinson, *ante*, p. 15.

by colonists long before the writing of The Declaration of Independence and The Constitution.[81]

It is certainly not realistic to go back to more than 250 years. But there is one statement applicable today: That the spirit of freedom, the rules of a republic, the developed democracy, and justice derived from the idea of natural law and a common sense living in a society of human beings is still vivid. The Declaration of Independence was clear in that sense.

Each American is part of the solution. We must raise consciousness around democracy. Is this lack of knowledge the underlying reason for people's disappointments and frustrations?

In the following chapter (Part 4) I would like to offer my heartfelt advice to all Americans who believe in the original meaning of American Democracy: a government truly *of* the people, *by* the people, and *for* the people.

81 Was this a consequence of the "Mayflower Compact" of November 1620? The settlers landing in Massachusetts travelling the Mayflower, signed this document to ensure a regulated life with functional social structure would prevail them from social chaos. It was a document declaring a self-governance system.

> "Life is never easy. There is work to be done and obligations to be met—obligations to truth, to justice, and to liberty."
>
> John F. Kennedy

Part 5: Review of the American Democracy

A Quiz for Democracy in the United States

Here is a quiz. Please evaluate how well we are acting to meet the following criteria for achieving true democracy (A is very well, D is awfully):

Formal criteria:

- Procedures set up in advance for Election Day A B C D
- Vote counting and vote data transfer A B C D
- Preparation and organization on Election Day A B C D
- Separation of Powers A B C D

Substance of democracy

- The attitude of politicians toward principles of democracy A B C D
- Treatment of democracy in the press A B C D
- Understanding of democracy by the Executive A B C D
- Understanding of democracy by Congress A B C D
- Understanding of democracy by the Supreme Court A B C D
- Understanding of democracy by the political parties A B C D
- Election propaganda A B C D

- Respect by politicians for other politicians A B C D
- Perception of other political ideas A B C D
- Willingness to compromise A B C D

Democracy as a political system; is there:

- Equality A B C D
- Reduction of the wage and income gap between rich and poor to a more and fair level A B C D

Civic understanding by all citizens

- Volunteering for needy causes A B C D
- Attitude toward paying taxes A B C D
- Trust in the services of the local government A B C D
- Confidence in the achievements of the State A B C D
- Confidence in Federal U.S. performance A B C D
- Expectations of the local government A B C D
- Expectations of the State A B C D
- Expectations of the Federal Government A B C D
- Feelings of nationality A B C D
- Willingness to take responsibility as Americans A B C D

You will find *my answers* on the website:

www.restore-our-democracy.com

Conclusive Call for Action

Considering the various facts outlined throughout this book and the companion book *RESTORE TRUST*, it should come as no surprise that I believe that American democracy is in poor shape. There is a widespread sentiment of malaise in the country, and changes are required to reduce the discomfort. So, what is next for America?

Ineffective politics can be revamped only when there is a political will to change. To begin with, it is important to find common ground and a strong intention to create change. The advantages of democracy are not offered freely; citizen action is necessary, such as supporting equal voting rights, becoming active in the political system, and reminding legislators of their campaign promises.

Here are some suggestions—simple, basic, yet with the potential to wake up society and help make a difference—for change. Remember that sometimes, a little bit goes a long way. A journey always begins with *a single first step.* It is up to you to take it.

How to Strengthen Democracy?

- **Commit to being an American citizen first, and only then a party member.**
- **Commit to being active in your local party.** Restore the concept of "government by the people, for the people." A democratic republic calls for the elected authority to mandate the will of the people. That is what we, as Americans, need to strive for and demand of our government.
- **Take part in all primaries, caucuses, and elections on State, Federal, and Community Level.**
- **Commit to setting up independent electoral commissions in each state** to abolish party wrangling, gerrymandering, and other voter restrictions with the understanding that the concerns and perspectives of the people must be represented equally in Congress. Gerrymandering, in particular, is fraudulent and must be abolished.

- **Act to abolish restrictions on voting.** Voting restrictions do not uphold the spirit of democracy—on the contrary, they destroy it! The fundamental requirement of good representation is still **"one person, one vote"** to have fair representations at all political levels.
- **Vote to support your values, not your dreams.** We must be more vigilant when electing officials. Learn to define your own needs, wants, and concerns and then vote for the candidates who will support those same needs and concerns. Trustworthy candidates are essential.
- **Do not blame, shame, or judge others**—try to think positively, make proposals, express your ideas, ask others for solutions, invite your follow citizens to discuss issues; make yourself a good example of how to engage in discussions capable of reaching compromises.
- **Again: It is a must to participate in elections.** Invite families and friends to go to the polls with you!
- Remember: **The American Declaration of Independence designed the vision of America as a nation defined by its commitment to the idea of equality. The American republic is based on virtues and moral ideals.**
- **Be in favor of regulating campaign financing;** big money must not influence the outcome of an election. Currently, members of Congress are being heavily influenced by big-money lobbyists. The promises made during campaigns must be kept by those elected.
- **Insist on participating in elections.** Ask your boss to give the time to vote. Ask friends and neighbors to give the needy rides to the polling station.

- **Support repealing the Citizens United vs. Federal Election Commission decision.** This Supreme Court ruling classifies corporations as people with rights under the Constitution to freedom of speech, and fails to place limits on campaign financing.
- **Be in favor of everyone paying fair taxes to local, state, and Federal authorities.** This will fund better infrastructure, good public schools, high security, and more.
- **Practice democratic thinking.** Everyone has to question opinions and statements asserting "facts" they know to be questionable in their everyday life.
- **Listen to other radio and TV programs than your usual ones.** You might catch some of your fellow Americans' ideas and broaden your political view.
- **Do everything possible to participate in elections. Take the day off to catch the opportunity to exercise your right as a citizen! Going to the ballot is an absolute must!**

Democracy as a structure of government is a principle that must protect everyone, even the less fortunate. The efforts it takes to strike a balance between rich and poor, between old and young, between the strong and the weak, between the big and the small, are huge and demanding.

What democracy is as a structure of government—an ideal target, an ideal attitude—is captured in many rules. Everyone in the country must know these rules and understand them as substance. Life according to these rules guarantees functioning in harmony and includes different requirements.

The law must promote equality. The law must support people. The law must lead to justice. The fulfillment of these ideals is a daily effort that can be called democracy.

Attachment 1: Voter Restrictions

Voting Rights

On Election Day, the whole eligible population of about 230 million Americans are invited to cast their votes to elect Congress. About half use their right.

Problems with Voter Registration

In **New Hampshire**, voters must register no later than 30 days prior to the election, on the grounds that presence in the state must be guaranteed.[82] The main victims of this restriction are the approximately 90,000 students whose residence in the state does not allow them to vote. That is 9% of the population.

In the state of **Texas**, proof of a "Texas license to carry a handgun", a weapon license, is recognized as an official document for voter registration.[83] Student IDs from universities in Texas are not recognized.

In 2018, 53,000 voter applications in **Georgia** were pending due to minor spelling and hyphenation errors in their documents

82 Casey McDermott, "N.H. Judge Blocks 'SB3' Voter Registration Law From Use In Upcoming Midterms", WBUR, October 22, 2018, available at http://www.wbur.org/news/2018/10/22/new-hampshire-sb3-voter-registration-law-blocked

83 Vote.org/voter-id-laws, Texas

and were initially not admitted to the poll.[84] A judge was able to lift the restraint three days before Election Day, but those affected had to prove their citizenship and eligibility to vote before Election Day, which was difficult or confusing for many. Seventy percent of these 53,000 citizens were Black.

In **Michigan**, the Secretary of State forgot to change the addresses of the voters' who had registered in 2018 but then moved, causing difficulties on Election Day.[85]

Between 2016 and 2018, **Arizona** offered the opportunity to register electronically as a voter by using a Driver's License. As many as 384,000 Arizona citizens registered for a change of residence and address in 2018, but these were not entered in the electoral register.[86] A few days before Election Day 2018, a Federal judge ruled that the Arizona agency's mistake in voter registration could not be corrected. Many of these voters saw their documents for the elections expire and they were not recognized for the elections.

---

84 Sean Keenan, "There are 53,000 pending voters in Georgia. They can still vote. Here's what you need to know", *Atlanta Magazine,* October 16, 2018, available at https://www.atlantamagazine.com/news-culture-articles/ 53000-pending-voters-georgia-still-vote-what-to-know/

85 Danielle Emerson, "MI Sec. of State Under Fire for Error Possibly Affecting Thousands", *Great Lakes Beacon*, October 19, 2018, available at http://greatlakesbeacon.org/2018/10/19/mi-secretary-of-state-under-fire-for-error-possibly-affecting-thousands/

86 Steven Rosenfeld, "How Arizona Officials May Obstruct Thousands of Voters". *The National Memo,* October 1, 2018, available at https://www.nationalmemo.com/how-arizona-officials-may-obstruct-thousands-of-voters/

Election List Clean Up

In the state of **Ohio**, the voter register was cleaned up in 2018. Voters who had not participated in two previous elections and had not returned a reply card were removed from the electoral register. Other voters who had not participated in the elections since 2008 had already been removed in 2015. Hundreds of thousands of citizens were affected.[87] Around 10% of voters belonging to a heavily African-American neighborhood were excluded in the Cincinnati area for the same reasons.[88]

This process of electoral rollover was approved in 2018 by the Supreme Court. This means that **Ohio**, like other states, has the right to manipulate the electoral roll and to exclude certain sections of the population—Black people in particular—from voting. The Brennan Center for Justice calculated that up to 16 million voters were excluded in various states.[89] The same electoral list adjustments were reported in **Georgia** and **Arizona**.

87 Andy Sullivan and Grant Smith, "Use it or lose it: Occasional Ohio voters may be shut out in November", Reuters, June 2, 2016, available at https://www.reuters.com/article/us-usa-votingrights-ohio-insight/use-it-or-lose-it-occasional-ohio-voters-may-be-shut-out-in-november-idUSKCN0YO19D

88 Jonathan Brater and others, "Purges: A Growing Threat to the Right to Vote" (New York: Brennan Center for Justice, 2018), available at https://www.brennancenter.org/publication/purges-growing-threat-right-vote

89 Jonathan Brater and others, *ibid.*

Strict Requirements for Voter ID Cards and Ballot Papers

On October 9, 2018, the U.S. Supreme Court supported a **North Dakota** state law that requires the voting card to provide the voter's home address.[90] Native Americans who live on reservations and only have mailboxes were particularly affected. The identity cards of around 30,000 American Indians were not accepted for election registration.

The state of **Kansas** requested in 2018 that proof of U.S. nationality must be presented. A Federal judge declared this invalid.[91] The law had required that voters fill out special ballot papers before entering the polling station; in this way voters who did not have the necessary documents were excluded from the election. Similar incidents were reported from **Alabama**, **Missouri,** and **Michigan**.

In **Alabama**, driving licenses were approved as meeting a requirement that voters provide a photo ID. In 2015, 31 Driver's License Offices were closed, thereby revoking many voters' right to vote because they could not get the necessary licenses.[92]

In **Georgia** and **Florida** in 2018, it was noted that absentee votes were not counted because the signatures did not exactly

---

90 Maggie Astor, "A Look at Where North Dakota's Voter ID Controversy Stands", *The New York Times,* October 19, 2018, available at https://www.nytimes.com/2018/10/19/us/politics/north-dakota-voter-identification-registration.html

91 Julie Bosman, "Judge Rejects Kansas Law Requiring Voters to Show Proof of Citizenship", *The New York Times,* June 18, 2018, available at https://www.nytimes.com/2018/06/18/us/kris-kobach-voting-fraud-lawsuit.html

92 Maggie Astor, "Seven Ways Alabama Has Made It Harder To Vote", *The New York Times,* June 23, 2018, available at https://www.nytimes.com/2018/06/23/us/politics/voting-rights-alabama.html

match those that were in the records of the authorities.[93] In **Georgia,** the law was subsequently invalidated.

Florida's Chairman of the Republican Party, Jim Greer, said in 2012, that early voting was restricted because it was not good for the party, and former Florida GOP leaders said voter suppression was the reason they pushed for the new election law.[94]

Former **North Carolina** local Republican activist Don Yelton remarked on voting restrictions, in 2012, including the requirement for a photo ID: "[We Republicans are] going to kick Democrats in the butt".[95] The Republican Party of North Carolina later vehemently rejected these statements, calling them "outrageous and intolerant", "completely inappropriate and offensive". The party declared that Mr. Yelton did not speak for the Republicans of his county and also demanded his resignation, which then took place. We cannot know to what extent Mr. Yelton spoke for many Republicans and to what extent these reactions were, therefore, more of a tactical nature, but it is very clear that the Republican Party is aware of how unjust such an attitude is.

U.S. District Chief Judge Mark Walker proclaimed in another case that arose about actions of county election officials in **Florida**:

> "This is a case about the precious and fundamental right to vote—the right preservative of all other rights. And it is

93 Amy Gardner, "Judge orders Ga. officials to stop tossing absentee ballots over signatures", *The Washington Post,* October 24, 2018, available at https://www.washingtonpost.com/politics/judge-orders-ga-officials-to-stop-tossing-absentee-ballots-over-signatures/2018/10/24/9c5a5b06-d7bd-11e8-a10f-b51546b10756_story.html?utm_term=.1988a4b464e7

94 Dara Kam, "Former Florida GOP leaders say voter suppression was reason they pushed new election law", *Palm Beach Post,* November 25, 2012

95 Jason Sattler, *ante*

about the right of a voter to have his or her vote counted. There is no doubt there must be election laws.... There is no doubt that election officials must make certain calls, under the rules, that deserve review. And there is no doubt some of those calls may hinge on highly subjective factors. The precise issue in this case is whether Florida's law that allows county election officials to reject vote-by-mail and provisional ballots for mismatched signatures—with no standards, an illusory process to cure, and no process to challenge the rejection—passes constitutional muster. The answer is simple. It does not."[96]

Voter Confusion Due to Administrative Errors and Misinformation

Another source of diminishing voter turnout is unsettling voters, intended or not. In **Massachusetts**, **Wisconsin,** and **New York**, various groups sent out messages that gave incorrect information about the polling locations, with the result that voters searched for wrong addresses and could not find the polling stations.[97]

In **Kansas**, false ballot papers were issued for a while.[98]

96 Cheyenne Haslett, "Judge sides with Nelson, rules Florida law on matching ballot signatures being applied unconstitutionally", ABC News, November 15, 2018, available at https://abcnews.go.com/Politics/judge-sides-nelson-rules-florida-law-matching-ballot/story?id=59214194

97 Max de Haldevang and Natasha Frost, "US voters are getting texts with false information about how and when to vote", *Quartz*, November 6, 2018, available at https://qz.com/1453215/midterms-voters-are-getting-texts-with-false-information-about-voting/

98 Lynn Horsley, Robert A. Cronkleton, and Aaron Randle, "Here are some of the problems Kansas and Missouri voters faced on Election Day", *The Kansas City Star*, November 6, 2018, available at https://www.kansascity.com/news/politics-government/election/article221167130.html

In **Montana**, the Republican National Committee incorrectly informed voters that a postal vote could still be made on the day of the election.[99] In contrast, the law specified completed ballot papers had to arrive by mail on the day of the election by 8:00 a.m.

Students from Prairie View A&M University, **Texas**, were asked by a local official to fill out an additional document, even though they were already registered voters.[100] The Texas Secretary of State declared the request incorrect, but confusion among potential voters had already occurred.

Voter Intimidation and Harassment

Idaho's White Supremacist group, Road to Power, made phone calls on behalf of the Democratic candidate in **Florida**[101] and made similar calls purportedly being made by Oprah Winfrey in **Georgia**[102] with pronounced racist and anti-Semitic slurs. Dis-

99 Eli Rosenberg, "The GOP mailed wrong information to voters in a Senate battleground. It says that was a mistake", *The Washington Post*, October 24, 2018, available at https://www.washingtonpost.com/politics/2018/10/25/gop-mailed-wrong-information-voters-senate-battleground-they-say-it-was-mistake/?utm_term=.1ed4778137e4

100 Matt Zdun, "Prairie View A&M University's voter registration issues are resolved, but voting barriers remain", *The Texas Tribune*, October 16, 2018, available at https://www.texastribune.org/2018/10/16/Prairie-View-voter-registration/

101 Jacey Fortin and Patricia Mazzei, "Racist Robocalls Target Andrew Gillum, Democratic Nominee for Florida Governor" , *The New York Times*, September 1, 2018, available at https://www.nytimes.com/2018/09/01/us/racist-robocall-andrew-gillum.html

102 Cleve R. Wootson, Jr., "Racist 'magical Negro' robo-call from 'Oprah' targets Stacey Abrams in Georgia governor's race", *The Washington Post*, November 5, 2018, available at https://www.washingtonpost.com/politics/2018/11/04/racist-magical-negro-robo-call-

paraging remarks by Republican Party support groups with racist and anti-Semitic references to Jewish candidates have been noted in **Alaska**, **North Carolina**, **California**, and **Pennsylvania**.[103] In **Missouri,** voters at ballot boxes were asked whether they were members of the Central America immigration caravan that was traveling from San Salvador to Mexico.[104]

Voters' intimidation came from the mouth of the President, who threatened severe punishments for fraud on Election Day.[105] Latinos in particular have been suspected of fraud. An unknown source issued a warning in the city of **Milwaukee**, **Wisconsin**, that the U.S. Immigration Service would check voters' IDs at polling stations, which the agency denied.[106]

Poll Closures and Long Lines

The opening hours of the polling stations are another point of controversy. Long queues indicate that voting is not smooth. For

---

oprah-targets-stacey-abrams-georgia-governorsrace/?utm_term=.e497e07d432e

103 Eli Rosenberg, "Republicans attack Jewish candidates across the U.S. with an age-old caricature: Fistfuls of cash", *The Washington Post*, November 6, 2018, available at https://www.washingtonpost.com/politics/2018/11/06/republicans-attack-jewish-candidates-across-us-with-an-age-old-caricature-fistfuls-cash/?utm_term=.00d29c10d205

104 Samantha Storey, "Voter Says Missouri Election Official Jokingly Asked If He Was 'Member Of The Caravan'", *HuffPost,* November 6, 2018, available at https://www.propublica.org/article/poll-worker-in-missouri-asks-if-voter-is-a-member-of-the-caravan

105 President Donald Trump, "7:41 a.m., November 5, 2018", *Twitter*, available at https://twitter.com/realDonaldTrump/status/1059470847751131138

106 Blake Paterson, "ICE, Dispelling Rumors, Says It Won't Patrol Polling Places", *ProPublica,* November 2, 2018, available at https://www.propublica.org/article/ice-dispelling-rumors-says-it-wont-patrol-polling-places

2012, the Joint Center for Political and Economic Studies calculated that around 730,000 voters were put off by the queues.[107] The Bipartisan Policy Center suspects that 3% of those waiting in the 2016 elections left the queue early.[108]

Since 2012, 214 polling stations have been closed in **Georgia**, most in areas with poor populations or either Black people, or other people of color.[109]

In Dodge City, **Kansas**, a polling station was set up far out of town, with no public transportation. Election officials contacted voters and assured them they could still vote in the old location—wrong information and an illegal practice.[110]

In **Florida**, a polling station in Deerfield Beach was moved to a gated community. When voters wanted to enter the area, guards stopped them.[111]

---

107 NAACP Legal Defense and Educational Fund, "Democracy Diminished: State and Local Threats to Voting Post-Shelby County, Alabama v. Holder" (2016), available at https://www.naacpldf.org/wp-content/uploads/Democracy-Diminished-State-and-Local-Threats-to-Voting-Post-Shelby-County-Alabama-v.-Holder.pdf

108 John C. Fortier and others, "Improving the Voter Experience: Reducing Polling Place Wait Times by Measuring Lines and Managing Polling Place Resources" (Washington: Bipartisan Policy Center, 2018), available at https://bipartisanpolicy.org/wp-content/uploads/2018/04/Improving-The-Voter-Experience-Reducing-Polling-Place-Wait-Times-by-Measuring-Lines-and-Managing-Polling-Place-Resources.pdf

109 Mark Niesse, Maya T. Prabhu, and Jacquelyn Elias, "Voting precincts closed across Georgia since election oversight lifted", *The Atlanta Journal-Constitution,* August 31, 2018, available at https://www.ajc.com/news/state–regional-govt–politics/voting-precincts-closed-across-georgia-since-election-oversight-lifted/bBkHxptlim0Gp9pKu7dfrN/

110 Tal Axelford, "New voters in Kansas town sent notices with wrong polling site", *The Hill,* October 25, 2018, available at https://thehill.com/homenews/news/413249-new-voters-in-kansas-town-sent-notices-with-wrong-polling-site

111 Daniel Rivero, "As Counties Place Polls In Gated Communities, Florida Voters Are Left Out", WLRN, November 6, 2018, available at

From **Texas**, **Illinois**, **Georgia**, and **Indiana**, it is reported that polling stations opened an hour later because there were not enough poll workers present.[112]

Malfunctioning Voting Equipment

Those who have finally managed to enter the right polling station with the right documents should be sure that their vote will go to the right party or candidate. But then, complaints about the voting machines are reported. In Texas, votes for Democrat Beto O'Rourke were credited to his opponent's account. Electoral officials' statement that it was a matter of voters' mistakes and not of the voting machines seemed implausible.[113]

Voting machine defects were reported in **Florida**, **Kansas**, **Maryland**, **Michigan**, and **New York** in 2018. Voting machine errors in **New York**, **North Carolina**, **South Carolina**, **Alabama**

---

http://www.wlrn.org/post/counties-place-polls-gated-communities-florida-voters-are leftout?fbclid=IwAR3gJOgXn5reXbhGWZu3PY_Lc ZNlonCaVIuLSAWnYW7QixoT1oJFys3To2M

112 Ian MacDougall and Ariana Tobin, "Long Lines Test Voter Patience Across the Nation", *ProPublica*, November 6, 2018, available at https://www.propublica.org/article/long-lines-test-voter-patience-across-the-nation; and CBS Chicago, "12 Northwest Indiana Polling Places To Stay Open Late", November 6, 2018, available at https://chicago.cbslocal.com/2018/11/06/porter-county-northwest-indiana-polling-places-open-late-election-day/; Juan Perez Jr., "Chicago officials report paper ballot problems, will keep 5 polling places open late", *Chicago Tribune,* November 6, 2018, available at https://www.chicagotribune.com/news/politics/elections/ct-met-chicago-election-day-problems-20181106-story.html

113 Andrea Zelinski, "Voting machine errors changed votes in Cruz-O'Rourke race, group says", *Houston Chronicle*, October 26, 2018, available at https://www.houstonchronicle.com/news/politics/texas/article/Voting-machine-errors-changed-some-Texans-13339298.php?t=35a415111e

and **Boston**, have been blamed on humidity or bad weather.[114] In **Arizona**, faulty printers were found responsible for missing ballot papers.[115] On Election Day 2018, around 1,800 voting machines in a **Georgia** warehouse were unused but had been intended for three election districts inhabited by supporters of the Democratic Party.[116] Other voting machines in Gwinnett County, **Georgia** lacked power cables.[117] The result: long queues and voters walking away.

---

114 Ian MacDougall, Jessica Huseman, and Isaac Arnsdorf, "Aging Machines, Crowds, Humidity: Problems at the Polls Were Mundane but Widespread", *ProPublica*, November 7, 2018, available at https://www.propublica.org/article/aging-machines-crowds-humidity-problems-at-the-polls-were-mundane-but-widespread; Andrew J. Yawn, "Jammed machines, cellphone ban, and other Election Day issues in Montgomery", *Montgomery Advertiser*, November 6, 2018, available at https://www.montgomeryadvertiser.com/story/news/politics/2018/11/06/2018-election-day-poll-issues-whats-jammed-machines-cell-phone-ban-and-other-election-day-issues-mont/1902816002/.

115 MacDougall, Huseman, and Arnsdorf, *ante*

116 Amy Gardner, Beth Reinhard, and Aaron C. Davis, "Brian Kemp's lead over Stacey Abrams narrows amid voting complaints in Georgia governor's race", *The Washington Post*, November 7, 2018, available at https://www.washingtonpost.com/politics/brian-kemps-lead-over-stacey-abrams-narrows-amid-voting-complaints-in-georgia-governors-race/2018/11/07/39cf25f2-e2b7-11e8-b759-3d88a5ce9e19_story.html?utm_term=.57b8d6b341cc

117 Michael King and Nick Sturdivant, "Gwinnett Co. voters wait for hours after workers forget power cords for the voting machines", WXIA-TV, November 6, 2018, available at https://www.11alive.com/article/news/politics/elections/gwinnett-co-voters-wait-for-hours-after-workers-forget-power-cords-for-the-voting-machines/85-611764666

Disenfranchisement of People Involved in Prior Criminal Actions

Finally, legal barriers must be reported that exclude groups of voters and deprive a considerable number of potential voters of their right to vote.

Uggen, Lasen, and Shannon report that six million Americans were excluded from voting for committing crimes and being in prison.[118] The question is, when can they get the right to vote again. Is it when they are released? When they have served their sentence? When they have paid all debts and fines? In **Alabama**, around 60,000 convicted citizens are affected.[119]

Citizens who are in pre-trial detention and who have not yet received a final judgment have been prematurely excluded from the right to vote in various states. Lawsuits have been filed against **Ohio** and **Indiana** authorities with respect to such voting restrictions.[120] The United States is known to have an extremely high prison rate.

---

118 Christopher Uggen, Ryan Larson, and Sarah Shannon, "6 Million Lost Voters: State-Level Estimates of Felony voting, 2016" (Washington: *The Sentencing Project*, 2016), available at https://www.sentencingproject.org/publications/6-million-lost-voters-state-level-estimates-felony-disenfranchisement-2016/

119 Maggie Astor, "Seven Ways Alabama Has Made It Harder To Vote", *The New York Times*, June 23, 2018, available at https://www.nytimes.com/2018/06/23/us/politics/voting-rights-alabama.html

120 Campaign Legal Center, "Ohio is Depriving Late-Jailed Citizens from Exercising Constitutional Rights, Lawsuit Says", Press release, November 6, 2018, available at https://campaignlegal.org/press-releases/ohio-depriving-late-jailed-citizens-exercising-constitutional-rights-lawsuit-says; and Harvard Law Review, "Thompson v. Alabama: District Court Finds No Irreparable Injury from the State's Lack of Notice to People with Felony Convictions upon Re-Enfranchisement", May 10, 2018, available at https://harvardlawreview.org/2018/05/thompson-v-alabama/

What are the Real Reasons for all the Restrictions?

In some cases, those responsible give the reasons why the electoral organization was structured in this way:

> "In North Hays County, students at Texas State University contacted county officials requesting extended voting hours and more voting locations after they were forced to wait in an hours-long line at the only on-campus polling place during the three days it was available. In response, the North Hays Republican party president sent an email saying that extended voting hours "probably means that it is going to favor the Democrats, so maybe I should not be in favor of this", while urging people to oppose extended polling hours for the nearly 40,000 college students at Texas State".[121]

The next closest polling place was located several bus rides away.[122] "We've got to cut down on early voting because early voting is not good for us".[123]

In the state of **Pennsylvania**, a new election law was enacted in March 2012, requiring specific photo identification for all voters. The bill was pushed by the majority party of the state (the

---

121 Aris Folley, "Texas college students allege voter suppression after GOP official calls for polling station to remain closed", *The Hill*, October 26, 2018, available at https://thehill.com/homenews/campaign/413330-texas-college-students-allege-voter-suppression-after-gop-official-calls

122 League of Women Voters of Texas, "After Facing Potential Litigation, Hays County Re-opens Texas State University On-Campus Polling Location", Press release, October 26, 2018, available at https://my.lwv.org/texas/article/after-facing-potential-litigation-hays-county-re-opens-texas-state-university-campus-polling

123 Jim Greer, "We've got to cut down on early voting because early voting is not good for us", *Palm Beach Post*, November 25, 2012

Republicans) and adopted by the Legislature. The official reason was to prevent electoral fraud.[124]

The Republican majority leader in the Pennsylvania House of Representatives, Mike Turzai, said, "the new Voter ID, which is gonna allow Governor Romney to win the state of Pennsylvania, done".[125] This election law was not applied due to objections in the 2012 election year and was repealed in 2014 as unconstitutional. However, the spirit of photo identification was still extant in 2016 when many voters were asked for a photo ID.[126]

The Republican Attorney General of **Texas,** and supporter of Greg Abbott's bid for state governor, said, "Their redistricting decisions were designed to increase the Republican Party's electoral prospects at the expense of the Democrats".[127]

Doug Preiss, the Chairman of the Republican Party in Franklin County (**Ohio**), observed that Republicans would fight early voting: "I guess, I really, actually feel we shouldn't contort the voting process to accommodate the urban—read African-American—voter-turnout machine".[128]

As a result of the many restrictions, there are fewer voters than there could be. The PEW Research Center reported that

---

124 Connor, Tracy (November 8, 2016). "Voters Wrongly Asked for ID at the Polls in Pennsylvania", NBC-News. Retrieved March 19, 2018

125 "Mackenzie Weinger, Pa.pol, Voter ID helps GOP win state," *Politico*, June 25, 2012 at http://www.politico.com/news/stories/0612/77811.html

126 Gerren Keith Gaynor, "Coalition files lawsuit against Pennsylvania voter ID law", *New Amsterdam Times* (New York), July 26, 2012

127 Ian Millhiser, "Texas Brags To Court That It Drew District Lines To 'Increase The Republican Party's Electoral Prospects'", *Think Progress*, August 14, 2013

128 Jason Sattler, *ante*

close to 2.2 million Americans were denied the opportunity to vote in the 2008 election.[129]

The list of voter suppression states is long: Alabama, Alaska, Arizona, California, Georgia, Illinois, Indiana, Kansas, Massachusetts, Michigan, Missouri, Montana, New Hampshire, New York, North Carolina, North Dakota, Ohio, Pennsylvania, South Carolina, Texas, and Wisconsin. They are spread all over the country. Twenty-one out of 50 states applied voter restrictions in 2016 and 2018. What is the reason?

Conclusion

With Gerrymandering still in place now, for 200 years, and with voter restrictions permanently and continually being applied to U.S. politics, there is one certain verdict: American citizens are not fairly represented! The failure of leaders and administrators to act with democratic understanding in all voting-related matters produces one-sided special interests—which is defined as plutocracy—the reign of the wealthy.

Governing a country is not a sports event with a winning and a losing team, but a process of compromising to make the entire population the winner.

129 The Pew Center on the States, "Upgrading Democracy: Improving America's Elections by Modernizing States' Voter Registration Systems", November 2010, in Mann/Ornstein, *ante, p.* 134

Amongst the novel objects that attracted my attention during my stay in the United States, nothing struck me more forcibly than the general equality of condition among the people. I readily discovered the prodigious influence which this primary fact exercises on the whole course of society; it gives a peculiar direction to public opinion, and a peculiar tenor to the laws; it imparts new maxims to the governing authorities, and peculiar habits to the governed.

I soon perceived that the influence of this fact extends far beyond the political character and the laws of the country, and that it has no less empire over civil society than over the government; it creates opinions, gives birth to new sentiments, founds novel customs, and modifies whatever it does not produce. The more I advanced in the study of American society, the more I perceived that this equality of condition is the fundamental fact from which all others seem to be derived, and the central point at which all my observations constantly terminated.

-Alexis de Tocqueville, *Democracy in America*

Attachment 2: Another View of Representation

View of the House of Representatives with Proportional Representation

When talking about Gerrymandering as voter fraud, one should know how many seats in the House of Representatives are actually affected. In this country, the majority voting system determines the outcome. The motto is: Winner takes all.

This principle leads to the division of constituencies, as only one party can win. The results of gerrymandered voting districts change the results in favor of the "organizing" party. It is incomprehensible and undemocratic. The intention of gerrymandering is to increase the number of seats to reach the goal of "Winner takes all".

The list below analyzes the distributions of seats proportionally to the number of voters. This is in contrast to the majority voting procedure where winner takes all.

A comparison of the voter shares of one of the two large parties with seats in Congress won by them shows a great imbalance in many states. This list compares the percentage of voters with the number of seats won in Congress. In the State of Alabama, to take the first state on the list, Democrats have a 34% share of the vote, but they only get 14.3% of the seats. The calculated difference of 19.7% would have to be compensated for by an additional seat, in which case the 34% share of voters would be balanced with a seat share of 28.6%. According to the proportional system, the Republican Party would have five seats, *i.e.,* 71.5% of the seats, with 66% of the vote.

The full list with all 50 States is published on the homepage:
www.restore-our-democracy.com

Please look up your State.

State	Total Seats f. State	Votes for D in %	Number Seats D	Part Seats in %	Diffe rence in %	Coef-fitient	Correc-tion D	Votes for R in %	Number Seats R	Part Seats in %	Diffe-rence in %	Coef-fitient	Correc-tion R
Alabama	7	34	1	14.3	-19.7	-1.38	1	66	6	85.7	19.7	1.38	-1
Alaska*	1	42	0	0	*	*	*	58	1	*	*	*	*
Arizona	9	45	4	44.4	-0.6	-0.05	0	55	5	55.6	0.6	0.05	0
Arkansas	4	13	0	0	-13	-0.52	0	87	4	100	13	0.52	0
California	53	64	39	73.6	9.6	5.08	-5	36	14	26.4	-9.6	-5.08	5
Colorado	7	50	3	42.9	-7.1	-0.5	0	50	4	57.1	7.1	0.5	0
Connecticut	5	64	5	100	36	1.8	-2	36	0	0	-36	-1.8	2
Delaware*	1	58	1	100	*	*	*	42	0	*	*	*	*
Florida	27	46	10	37	-9	-2.42	2	54	17	63	9	2.42	-2
Georgia	14	40	4	28.6	-11.4	-1.6	2	60	10	71.4	11.4	1.6	-2

* Majority Vote with one seat only

Biography

Werner Neff holds a PhD in Political Science and a Master's Degree in Economics. Deeply passionate about Democracy, political science, and economics, Neff has researched and written several books on social economy and politics during the past 10 years. ***RESTORE OUR DEMOCRACY*** fulfills on his long-time dream of writing a book on the principles of Democracy, as his contribution to the future.

Neff, a Swiss citizen married to an American, has been living in the mountains of Colorado for over 10 years. He loves the American people and is deeply invested in their wellbeing, and that of the country, as well; this book is meant as a contribution and inspiration to both. It is his fondest wish that the history and democratic principles, as well as his conclusive call for action, will help strengthen our resolve to return to the fundamental values of Democracy.

Bibliography

The list of books and articles used in this text is published on the homepage of:

www.restore-our-democracy.com